THE SPACE OF THE WAIST®

Follow THE SPACE OF THE WAIST® on:
Website/Blog - www.thespaceofthewaist.com
Facebook - www.facebook.com/thespaceofthewaist and
Pinterest - www.pinterest.com/christamelody/the-space-of-the-waist

BOOK 18:

HOURGLASS BODY SHAPE WITH A SHORT WAIST

Book 18: The Hourglass Body Shape with a Short Waistplacement, along with *The Guide Book* and all other books within the series for our Body Shape and THE SPACE OF THE WAIST® are available on:
www.amazon.com/author/melodyedmondson

C. Melody Edmondson, Msc.D.
MJP ©2015

Published by MJP Publishing Inc., 2015
Attn. Melody Edmondson 12112 N. Rancho Vistoso Blvd. Tucson, AZ. 85755 | email: thespaceofthewaist@gmail.com

Library of Congress Cataloging-in-Publication Data
10 9 8 7 6 5 4 3 2 edition
Copyright © 2015. All rights reserved.
Edmondson, Melody

Book 18 - Hourglass Body Shape with a Short Waist
Lexicon and Indices for complete book series included in Book 1 - *The Guide Book:* Your Fashion Guide Based on your Body Shape and THE SPACE OF THE WAIST®

CREDITS
Book Copy Editing by Simone Gers and Sandy Marie.
Cover Design, Interior Formatting/Layout, and Figure Illustrations by David A. Russell via Studio DRive C_ | www.studiodrivec.com

NOTICE
Without limiting the rights under copyright reserved above, no part of this publication may be reproduced, stored in or introduced into a retrieval system, or transmitted, in any form or by any means (electronic, mechanical, recording, photocopying, or otherwise) without the prior written permission of both the copyright owner and the above publisher of this book. Request to the Publisher for permission should be addressed to: Attn. Melody Edmondson 12112 North Rancho Vistoso Blvd. Suite A-150 Tucson, AZ. 85755 or via email at thespaceofthewaist@gmail.com

The scanning, uploading, and distribution of this book via the Internet or any other means without the permission of the publisher is illegal and punishable by law. Please purchase only authorized electronic editions and do not participate in or engage electronic piracy of copyrighted materials.
Your support of the author's rights is appreciated.

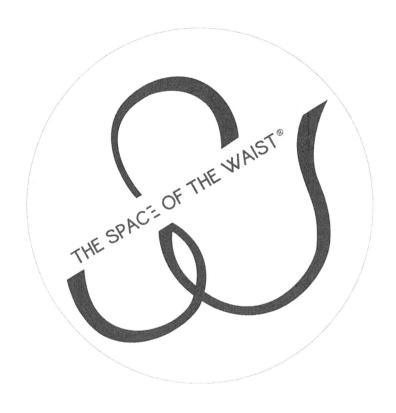

DEDICATION TO MY MOTHER

The Guide Book and its series of eighteen books, including this book, are dedicated to my beautiful, creative Mother, Marilyn Grace McClure Place.

With her belief and consistent encouragement throughout my lifetime, I stretched my boundaries and accomplished what I have. Without her steadfast ethical and spiritual inner grace, I never would have found my inner peace. Without her generosity, highly creative spirit, know-how, and her unfailing love, I am not sure I could have survived the outside world, as a sensitive.

Also, I never would have known about the fairies who lived in the clover nor the angels who slept in my top bunk. I may not ever have had such deep appreciation for all of God's many ways of helping. Mother had a great imagination, and it was a gift to her children.

Mother encouraged us each wholeheartedly and believed in each of us. I was shown I had value and to TRUST my inner voice, my inner guidance; Mother called this conscience. God is the ultimate adviser of the Self. Mother believed God was everywhere. We were to rely on *this* forever guidance.

Through Mother's loving presence, special regard, her inherent belief in God, her ability to create beauty wherever she goes, her many talents, her personal inner and outer beauty and her sincere devotion to me, I acknowledge my "Blessed Gift" of my unique mother, and I dedicate this book and the book series to my mother, Marilyn Grace McClure Place.

SECTIONS LIST

Dedication to My Mother

Sections List / List of Illustrations

Acknowledgements

Introductions - The Guide Book Overview and Goal,
The Hourglass Body Shape With a Short Waistplacement = Hourglass S

Quick Review (Refer to Book 1 - The Guide Book for more details, including Lexicon and Indices)

Good Ideas that Flatter the Hourglass S Body Shape

Create-a-Coat Canvas of Wearable Art

Backdrop Dressing

Information by Key Classifications for Your Silhouettes

Transform/Refresh a Garment into a Wearable Silhouette

General Ideas to Avoid if you are an Hourglass S

Celebrities/Models With Hourglass Body Shape & Short Waistplacement

Shape-Shifters for Hourglass S

Advanced Illusion *Shape-Shifters* for Hourglass S

Building Your Basic Black Trans-Seasonal Wardrobe (Basic 57)

Formulas for Hourglass S = S4, S3, S2, and S1

Shopping Lists/Recap of Best Silhouettes for Hourglass S

Author Bio

ILLUSTRATIONS LIST

A complete list of all illustrations organized by Sections List. All figures illustrated by David A. Russell.

How to Measure for Waistplacement - EMWP: Figure 1a

Female Body Shape - Hourglass S: Figure 1b

Wearable Art Coat Canvas: Figures 2 - 8

Backdrop Dressing: Figures 9 - 45

Shape-Shifters: Figures 46 - 52

Advanced Illusion *Shape-Shifters*: Figures 53 - 67

Layering Formulas/Line Break Examples: Figures 68 - 71

"There is usually a way to adapt a fashion trend for your Body Shape and Waistplacement. But...when it comes to daily dressing, IT IS your WAISTPLACEMENT not seasonal trends and not your weight that is the defining factor for your clothing selections."

- C. Melody Edmondson

ACKNOWLEDGEMENTS

I wish to express my deep gratitude to the special people who made this book possible. Without their expertise and support, I would not have been able to properly execute *The Guide Book* and the 18 books within *THE SPACE OF THE WAIST® book series*.

Thank you to the *sacred* Simone Gers for editing *The Guide Book* and some of the books within *The Book Series*. Simone also made contributions to all of the books within *The Book Series*. Simone's suggestions led to the development of a separate book, *The Guide Book,* and each of the Body Shapes by Waistplacement books, standing alone as individual books, versus an all-in-one book. Simone has taught me much and not just about book writing.

Thank you to my dear friend, Sandy Marie, for the final editing of *The Book Series*, to include *The Guide Book*. Also, special thanks to Sandy, for being such a beautiful fashion ICON, artist and an inspiration to all fashionistas.

Most importantly, I have been blessed to have had the technologically savvy, David A. Russell owner and Creative Director of Studio DRive C_, as my Cover Designer, Illustrator and Production Manager for *The Guide Book* and *The Book Series* (18) expressing THE SPACE OF THE WAIST®. David is talented beyond what space could allow.

THE SPACE OF THE WAIST®

The Guide Book is the first book in the series and should be read first, in order for you to discover or **verify** your Body Shape & Waistplacement.

"**THE SPACE OF THE WAIST®**" will help you find your unique Body Shape and your personal **WAISTPLACEMENT** which determines how *much* space is available in your waist area. This knowledge provides valuable insight into your clothing, fashion, Silhouette and accessory choices. ***Waistplacement*** is essential to style/garment/apparel or what I refer to as **SILHOUETTE** selection as the waist modifies the Body Shape very dramatically. Once you discover if you are Balanced, Short or Long-waisted, your selections become easy.

Body Shape correlated to Waistplacement is uncovered territory at the Wholesale, Manufacturing and Retail Store levels of the Women's Apparel Industry. It is time for an **INDUSTRY CHANGE.** Once women demand Long-waisted and Short-waisted clothing/apparel in their Silhouette choices, the **Retailers** will encourage and inform the Designers and Manufacturers in the Apparel Industry and The Fashion World will transform. Consumer demand will get the ball rolling in the 21st Century. My goal for Retail Store availability of Short and Long Waist Silhouettes by classifications is 2018 or soon thereafter.

Now that you have read Book One: *The Guide Book* and have downloaded/purchased the proper book for your individual Body Shape with its associating Waistplacement, you can begin to learn how to best flatter your Body Shape and Waistplacement. Your best Silhouettes, tips for layering, and the building of your Basic Black Wardrobe in Trans-Seasonal Fabrics are provided. Also included, is a guide to *your* Shopping Cycles & Shopping List/Recap.

HOW TO MEASURE FOR THE SPACE OF THE WAIST®

The Easy Measure Waistplacement (EMWP):
I have provided a simple method: "The Easy Measure Waistplacement" or EMWP. To determine your Waistplacement, measure from right at the bottom of your bra band to the smallest nipped-in place of the waist (See the illustration below on the EMWP measurement technique).

On an average woman of 5 feet 4 inches through 5 feet 10 inches:
* NOTE: Measurement Conversion .3 = 5/16 inch.
    Patternmakers usually grade 1/6" to 1/8" from size 8 up or down the sizes.
- A Balanced Waistplacement measurement is 6.3 to 7 inches.
- A Long Waistplacement is any measurement over 7 inches.
- A Short Waistplacement is any measurement under 6.3 inches.

If you are under 5 feet 4 inches tall, your numbers are nearer to 4.3 inches to 5 inches for Balanced Waistplacement; therefore, if you are under these numbers you are Short-waisted. If you are over these numbers, then you are Long-waisted.

If you are over 5 feet 10 inches in height, Balanced Waist Measurement becomes 8.3 to 9 inches. If your measurement is shorter, you are Short-waisted. If your measurement is longer, you are Long-waisted.

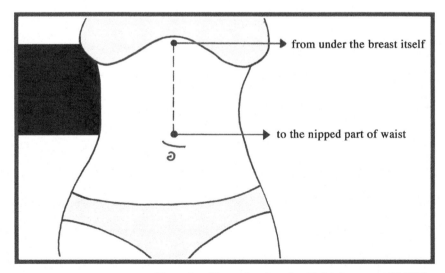

Figure 1a - Measuring Area for Waistplacement (EMWP)

HOURGLASS BODY SHAPE WITH A SHORT WAIST = HOURGLASS S

This Body Shape is within the *family* of the longtime favorite Hourglass B "Ideal" Shape. The Hourglass S Body Shape has a shorter Waistplacement; hence, Hourglass Short-Waisted. Hourglass S has fewer inches in THE SPACE OF THE WAIST®. With this Short Waistplacement your measurement from bra band to the nipped in Waist is less than 6.3 to 7-inches. Wear your best "hold up the breasts" bra when you measure. This uplift gives you more space in the Waist. THE SPACE OF THE WAIST may be only 3 or 4-inches versus the 6.3 to 7-inches for a Balanced Waistplacement. Your Shoulders and Hips are approximately the same width and your Waist *is* 8-10 inches smaller than your hips and shoulders. However, as a gift, your *legs are usually much longer* than most of the other Hourglasses. Longer legs are one of Nature's many balancing acts in creating us equally; we each have our physical, mental, and spiritual GIFTS.

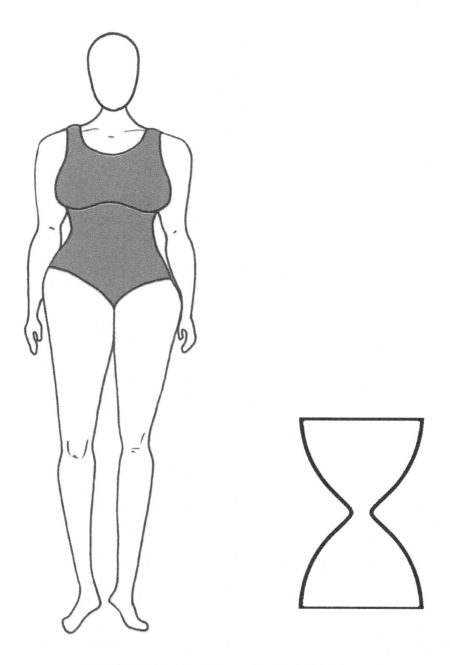

Figure 1b - Hourglass Body Shape with a Short Waistplacement

QUICK REVIEW

The **UNCHANGEABLES** and Primary Modifiers of the Body Shape are height and Waistplacement. Other UNCHANGEABLES that are not *primary* in modifying the Body Shape are neck, leg or arm length, foot or hand size, leg shape, ankle, or bone size.

Your Body Shape includes **Secondary Modifiers or CHANGEABLES** of the Body Shape. Body size and its BMI in terms of a *"variable"* may fluctuate and is one of these ***Changeables.***

All women have **internal and external *Assets*** on which you can focus. Examples of these visual/physical ***Assets*** to feature are slimmer arms, smaller ankles, shapely calves, longer neck, wonderful hair, glorious skin, great teeth, beautiful eyes, a bright addictive smile or a pretty face. Focus on your ***Assets*** to feature them through your clothing looks, Silhouettes, colors/pigments and accessories.

Inner ***Assets*** to feature and highlight might be slightly more abstract, including artistic nature, sense of humor, intelligence, interests, femininity, intelligence, edginess, subtle sexiness and inner beauty to name just a few. Keep in mind your personality, soul and essence when making clothing selections. Every woman has her own unique ***Style Aesthetic***. For the purpose of this book, let us return to dressing the *whole self* as well as the body with its Waistplacement.

The Waistplacement may be Short, but the varieties of Body Shape are many. You may have a small to large bustline or a small to large buttocks. Bone sizes and height come in many varieties. Most Short-Waisted women have longer legs, most *Long-Waisted* women have shorter legs and most Balanced Waisted women have average length legs regardless of Body Shape. Enjoy, as a Short-Waisted woman, your gift of longer legs. There will be Hourglass S figure variances in women. Some women may have wider and or flatter buttocks and/or flatter chests, but none-the-less they are Hourglass S. their legs may be shorter or they may be flatter in body depth than the known "Ideal" Hourglasses. Some examples of the Ideals are: Marilyn Monroe (B), Elizabeth Taylor (B), Scarlett Johannsen (B), Sofia Vergara (B), Salma Hayek (B), and Sophia Loren (L).

GOOD IDEAS IN GENERAL IF YOU ARE HOURGLASS S

Value your *Assets* and feature them.

Keep in mind, if you are *not too* Short-Waisted, 3/4 to 1-inch Short-Waisted, you could wear a lower slung trouser with a matching or same-toned belt and get away with it. If you are too Short-Waisted, however, it looks unattractive. If your hips are directly under your waistline, have higher hips, do not try this, as it will simply focus on the widest part of the body. Wearing a slimmer tunic with stretch will be a better option for all Short-waisted women. Likewise, it is better to forget the tuck-ins altogether. A tucked in blouse or sweater into: a jean, trouser or skirt is an unflattering look. Wearing these tuck-ins, anything belted at the Waist and **anything** fitted at the Waist such as a dress, coat, top, or gown will not be becoming on any Short-waisted Hourglass (IN FACT, any Short-Waisted woman). These fitted at the Waist Silhouettes create width and depth, making you visually appear shorter and heavier in size. It is a good idea to begin to love and admire straightlines in coats, dresses, jackets, gowns and tops while an Hourglass S. Keep colors monochromatic or dark in pigmentation to elongate the Body Shape.

ONE WAY TO REVEAL THE WAISTLINE:
Defining the Waistline while Short-waisted is very difficult to execute attractively. The best manner in which to succeed with this look is through a knitted body-conscious dress. The knit contours to your Natural Body Shape, whether in tops, dresses, or gowns. All other fitted at the Waist dresses, gowns, jackets, and tops will not be visually attractive on a Short-waisted woman due to her widening effect and the adding of visual weight to the body. The proportion fitted at the waist Silhouettes create by emphasizing the too Short Waist and short length from bust to waist is not attractive. There is not enough space in the waist.

The best dresses for Short-waisted Hourglasses are the straightlined and no-Waist dresses such as chemises, shifts, sheaths and floats. The Dropped-waisted Silhouette in maxi skirts and dresses work beautifully, because they not only camouflage the Waistplacement, but also have longer interesting skirt bodies. Most Short-waisted women have longer legs; therefore, most Hourglass S may wear the maxi, midi, and ankle lengths beautifully.

Knits and matte jersey are good ways to be able to rock your curves. Hip belts may be worn but none at the waist. Cutting the body in half with a waist belt only makes the body appear wider and shorter. This fact is regardless of your weight. The hip belt is a good idea as it skews the waist and is a great way to wear a belt for most all Short-Waisted woman, especially Hourglass S.

Successful dressing dictates that curves are shown subtly, rather than emphasized. Wearing knits daily would become tiresome, so for variety, include linear lines, straightlines, no-waisted and Dropped-waist Silhouettes. Artsy-dressing and architectural designs with linear movement are novel ways to dress and create interesting looks. If you are wider and/or deeper, these are also great choices. Be careful of their detail placement in order to control the widening or bulking effects they could create on your body.

Wear longer, leaner black tanks as your bottom-layering item. This will become a wardrobe staple for Short-waisted women. This underlayer-tank represents the most, immediate relocation of the Waist. Visually, through the longer line of the bottom layer tee-shirt, the eye moves to the lower-hip and toward your amazing long legs which are an *Asset.* In this way, the eye flows in a longer line, versus concentrating on the Waist area. Through this camouflaging of the Waistplacement, the focus is drawn toward your *Assets.* This bottom layer tank helps elongate the Waist, and in a contrasting color, it could further accentuate the lower hipline creating a more vivid eyebreak at the lower hip or thigh area. The longer, leaner black stretch-tank worn over a minimizer will be a standard way of life for you as Hourglass S Body Shape. I for one know this first hand, as I am an Hourglass S. It will forever elongate and skew the Waistplacement.

Keep ALL of your tops, jackets, dresses, and gowns without fitted tight bodices and make sure that they do not fit at the Waistline. Keep fitted items, of any variety, away from the Waistline, except in knits. This is *key information* for jackets, dresses, gowns, and blouses in particular. Wear knitted dresses and tops, wear knitted or straightlined jackets that are wrist length or longer. You may add long necklace layers or longer scarves in order to visually elongate and subtly show off your beautiful curves. In this way, the Waistplacement is not as pronounced because it is skewed by the accessories and contour of the knitted fabrics. It would be VERY pronounced if you were to wear a dress or coat with a belt at the Waist. It is most always best (unless very minimally Short-Waisted 3/4 to 1-inch) to NOT wear a fitted at the Waist ANYTHING! This is the most important knowledge to acquire for any Short-waisted Body Shape. The fitted Silhouettes in jackets, coats, dresses, gowns and tops are not the correct selections for your Wardrobe. This is something that will never change, regardless of your weight. Short-waisted means, you have an **UNCHANGEABLE WAISTPLACEMENT.** Now is the right time to get your closet cleaned out and freed of all the wrong Silhouettes for your Waistplacement. Get organized for your true lifelong self, and to realign your shopping needs to accommodate the body you have not the body you thought you had, or the one you thought you could obtain through dieting. Your Waistplacement will never move lower, so equip yourself with the proper knowledge to choose the right Silhouettes for your Waistplacement and Body Shape.

Eye movement is best when it has a linear or curvilinear flow.
Linear: from the face, hair, neck to the shoulders and bustline, then flowing to the lower-hip near the wrists, to the long legs and the bottom of the shoe. (Shoes in stilettos or higher heels are best).
Curvilinear: From the face, hair, bustline, hipline, waistline, thigh-line, knee-line to the shoe then back to the face, and repeat. Hourglass S will use **Linear flow of eye movement** more often due to camouflaging the Waistplacement. On occasion, she will use the **Curvilinear flow of eye movement** when selecting a knitted body-conscious, body-contouring dress that reveals the shorter Waistline but has a distinct curving flattering, sexy flow. By wearing knitted, tighter tops under a longer and heavier, knitted, straightlined jacket, Hourglass S can achieve a curvilinear line.

Do not confuse Hourglass with the Inverted Triangle. See the illustrations in Book 1 - *The Guide Book* of the Inverted Triangle Body Shape. Seek photos online of the 1980-1990's top model, Elle Mac Pherson, and celebrities, Charlize Theron and Catherine Zeta Jones, who both have narrow hips and broader shoulders. This is visually obvious because the shoulders are wider by 4-inches (plus) than their narrow hips. Some women with an Inverted Triangle Body Shape and larger breasts, *think* that they are Hourglass. They are confused because of the fuller bustline and because of their wider shoulders. However, their waist is not 10-inches smaller than the hips. The Inverted Triangle usually has larger natural breast and wider shoulders. The confusion is in having the top-half as an Hourglass yet not the curvy bottom-half of an Hourglass. The inverted Triangle bodies are slimmer hipped and with a smaller and flatter buttocks. They are in general straighlined from waist downward versus curvy as Hourglass. They believe that they are a slim Hourglass shape, but instead they are Inverted Triangle, whether they are tall or short. There are many tips in Inverted Triangle Book for the top half of the body if you Borderline both Hourglass and Inverted Triangle S. You may download both books. (Review Book 1 - *The Guide Book* for measurement methods).

If you are a narrow, average or wider and deeper Hourglass S, the no-Waist dress idea is always wise as it visually elongates your Body Shape. Select Silhouettes such as a chemise, float, sheath or shift. Dropped-waisted Silhouettes are also very flattering. We need many more of these Dropped-waisted day-dresses and skirts available for purchase.

It is a good idea to elongate the shape by wearing linear and straight lines; use the advantage available today in linear color blocking and color shaping *Shape-Shifters*. These dresses and tops (mostly dresses) have superimposed upon the dark grounds of the dress the Hourglass curves. Some are merely linear, versus curvy, color panels. The straighter panels also create a linear eye flow and elongate and narrow the Body Shape. Selecting the Hourglass panel option in *Shape-Shifters*, will further add *curve* to the Body Shape.

Undergarments and minimizers/shapers play a major role in creating a foundation for a dress, gown, coat, trouser, skirt, jacket, and top to fit the body better. Bras that up-lift the breasts to a higher position lengthen THE SPACE OF THE WAIST®. Another great idea is to wear, full length, stretch shapers such as a long-lined tank with full sized stretch panties. Another idea is a long-lined, tight yet stretchy shaper in a length that covers the knees. If you can find one, the shapers in stretch to the ankles, are wonderful. The tight stretch fabric of any of the shapers/minimizers, holds the body tight, so the garments worn over them slide over the body more easily. These stretchy shapers also remove any lumps or bumps created by BMI. If you are older, they also hold tight the aging sags created by years on planet Earth and its much-needed gravity. Also, always wear a good support bra to raise the breasts in order to give yourself that extra needed "Space of the Waist."

Keep femininity alive through ruffled edges on sweaters, skirts some jackets and dresses. Do not overpower the figure and be very conscious where the details are placed, as they could be adding width, depth or shortness to your waist. The idea is to elongate, not shorten, the upper body and in this manner you balance it with your long legs.

Glamour is associated with Hourglass whether you are a glamorous girl/women or not, it is good to play with glamour through your looks. It does not have to be in a dressy manner but through dressy items mixed with your everyday clothing items like jeans and leather. This is alternative glamour and is best expressed through high-low dressing (mixing expensive items with non-expensive items in one look), and juxtaposition (mixing out of character items together in one look such as a ball gown skirt with a heavy sweater and flat, studded biker boots and a leather jacket). Both are good methods of dress. Be creative and have fun with your looks, while at the same time, camouflaging where your Natural Waistplacement resides.

Be careful not to over layer your clothing as this adds bulk. You may purchase tops and dresses today that are self-layered. These are a novel and stellar invention.

Weight is evenly distributed all over the body on Hourglass S. Weight gain is also all over, versus in distinct areas. No one will know the difference so carry on!

Venture into geometrically shaped dresses/coats/jackets/tops for fun, novelty and yes camouflaging the Waistplacement. Rock those long legs, bustline, face, hair, personality, smile, or inner beauty.

It is a great idea to look for artsy styled clothing with flat Waistlines. Look for asymmetry and irregular shapes that are linear in line. Easy layering pieces such as narrow and longer tunics, tops, tee-shirts, shirts, jackets and coats are good choices. Asymmetrical hemlines on linear trousers, jeans, skirts, dresses, coats, or jackets are a fun and interesting option. Search for unique artsy retail stores all over the world, in the comfort of your home via the Internet, or seek them out in your hometown and support your local community.

Be aware you always have options other than the fitted and flared and fitted at the waist dresses, as these Silhouettes are not an option for you. Your options will be sheaths (if toned, slimmer or muscular), shifts, chemises, floats (Silhouettes that are not too wide and not shirred as shirring adds width and depth to the body), and **straightlined** coats, dresses, gowns, jackets, or tops. Your go-to sportswear-separates are longer black jackets, longer, fitted and flared trousers and jeans with tops left on the outside. Wear belts at the hip versus the Waist. The jackets must be straightlined with no nipped-in-waist! Straight cut knits are great as well as the body-conscious knits.

Be aware of artsy and geometrically shaped garments in stiff fabrics that are oversized. You may need to have them narrowed. It is common for Hourglasses to need larger sizes to accommodate the bustline and/or shoulders, making them too big elsewhere. The sleeve may also be too long in the cuff. It is necessary for all Hourglasses to have a skilled seamstress to make your many needed alterations.

Linear lines are a good idea to elongate the overall bodyline. You may select a longer and leaner tunic or menswear shirting Silhouette in order to camouflage the Waistplacement by wearing a top on the outside of the trousers, jeans or skirts. You may opt to belt at the lower hip or not belt at all. Leaner jackets or tops in lower hip-length elongate the Waistplacement the best. Wear tops, jackets and the bottoms of skirts/trousers/jeans all in the same color pigment. The idea is to lengthen the Body Shape, minimize the width and not to add depth to the Body Shape.

Keep in mind you may factor *your own* input and personal experience into the selections where you have had success. If you are a narrower Hourglass, you have more options than if you are a wider Hourglass. When this wider/narrower issue skews your Silhouette or other choices, it will be indicated in parenthesis in **The Shopping List/Recap.**

A higher neckline may be worn when wearing a dress without a defined Waist. Undefined Waists are Silhouettes such as a chemise, columns, float, sheath or a shift dress. These higher necklines such as crew neck, jewel, round, high neck, or mock turtleneck elongate the upper body and skew the Waistplacement, as the bodyline becomes the neckline to the hemline. Due to the fact that the Waistline is camouflaged, the overall effect is a longer and leaner Body Shape. If you wear these all in the same-color-pigment and wear a maxi skirt, dress or full-length gown, the bodyline becomes neckline to floorline, elongating the bodyline ever further. However, if you have a shorter neck a vee-ed neckline may be better. Check your personal Gestalt. The width of the body and the length of the neck determine if higher necklines will flatter you or make your neck look shorter. Often if the bustline is very large, higher necklines do not work, as you look fuller in the top due to the Short Waist. If you have a long neck there is more length to the line, being from neckline to hemline. Certainly V-eed, sweetheart, scoops and U-necklines are most always a wise choice for Hourglass S.

Fail-Safe Silhouettes and looks: Wear a dress that is below-the-knee, with a v-eed neckline, elbow-length sleeves, that is either a knitted, body-conscious sheath, chemise, float, or shift Silhouette. In sportswear the Fail-Safe looks are: black, longer, leaner jackets (with no nipped-in waists but with a straight-cut), fitted and flared trousers and jeans, longer and leaner tank-tops with another top layered over it in a leaner, longer length (all worn over the minimizer). Pencil or stitched-down-pleated skirts (all worn with longer leaner tops layered over the Waistband of the bottom [trouser, jean, or skirt] to at least the lower hip or longer). Wear the above looks with black opaques, black stilettos and high-heeled leather or suede shoes. Remember, in order to best elongate the bodyline, the shoe toe must show underneath the trouser or jean flares; hence, the pointed-toe shoe. Opt for bare legs and skin-toned/nude pigment shoes, boots, or booties when opaques are not trending or in season.

If your occasion dictates wearing flat shoes, select your flats with pointed-toes, as they will elongate the legs and your proportion the best. Stacked heeled boots/pumps work if the heel is not too thick and heavy (thickness tends to draw you closer to the ground and makes you appear shorter and wider). Heavy shoes draw the eye downward. Decide if this is what you want or do you wish to feature other *Assets*? If your legs are thicker, more muscular or shorter, these heavier shoes, boots, sandals only make your legs appear thicker versus streamlined. If you desire or need to wear flats, there are many Silhouettes on the market today with lighter more feminine flair. With a strong calf, a wedge or platform shoe, boot, booties, or sandal may be worn, but think about where the eye will flow and if that is your most flattering option. There are wedges in daintier, unbulky Silhouettes today, select from amongst *those* for the most flattering Silhouettes. Rounded toes also work.

Longer leaner trousers and jeans with deep Dark Pigment jackets, sweaters/tops are best in all the same (or near the same) color. If you are a wider and/or a deeper Hourglass, then color choice is essential for elongation. It is a good idea to show skin when possible, if you have worked hard in the gym, or through genetics, happen to have the luxury of longer, leaner or toned arms and legs. Feature your arms and legs if they are *ASSETS.*

You have many Assets. If your bustline is an *Asset,* feature it in U, V-eed, or Sweetheart necklines. Enjoy variations in your necklines, sleeve Silhouettes, sleeve lengths, shoulder styles, and coat, skirt, dress, and gown lengths. **Rock your legs!**

Having a defined shoulder is a great idea for Hourglass S. To develop impact, add Shoulder pads. There are many varieties of shapes and depths in shoulder pads today. They are available online. They may be inserted into your tops, dresses, gowns, jackets, coats, to add width and stature to the shoulders. Have a seamstress add snaps to the pads, and add the holders in the proper location inside your clothing Silhouettes. You may change and alternate the pads for your shoulder styles. Be sure the seamstress attaches all snaps and snap-holders at the same spacing or alternating of various shoulder pad types does not work. Use smaller or larger ones for variety. Adding novel shoulders from time to time totally changes a LBD, tops, dresses, jackets and gowns.

Softly padded bras can add enhancement to the bustline. If you are one of the fewer smaller busted Hourglass Body Shapes with lower BMI.

Details need to be kept to a minimum. But subtle details such as hemlines on jackets, dresses, coats, tops, gowns, skirts or trousers are wonderful and feminine when either fluted, ruffled, lettuced edges, faggotted or with tiny pleating details.
Revealing the arms as well as the legs if you are slender, muscular or toned can help to visually created eye movement, sexiness and femininity to your look.

If your buttocks is very small you may opt for a padded panty-shaper with not only buttocks but hip enhancements. Padding creates an even more obvious Hourglass Body Shape for the lower BMI Hourglasses. You may also select trousers or jeans with added flaps or details on the pockets as they tend to round the buttocks and help it to appear lifted and rounded in jeans, trousers, dresses, skirts, and gowns.

COLOR, PRINT, PATTERN AND GROUNDED PRINTS/PATTERNS IN SPACED-OUT DESIGN CHOICES:

It is easy to select from your *key* Basics and put together a layered look. This black canvas creates a backdrop for your themes or accessories and jewelry accents. These accessories may be used to express your personality through metaphoric selections. They may also be skillfully layered in order to improve your bodyline.

Monochromatic dressing in Darker Pigments, or same-scale color pigments, is the best idea for all Hourglass S as they elongate the Body Shape. If you are wider and/or deeper also select dark on dark, such as navy and black, or dark gray and black, as Dark Pigment color combinations add variety to your looks and reveal your Natural curves.

If you are a narrow, very tall, and also smaller chested Hourglass S, you may select Lighter Pigmentations without any enlargement or bulk to the Body Shape. But for the average and wider and/or deeper Hourglass S, Darker Pigments elongate the Body Shape the best.

Black is always a safe color choice. When in doubt choose black pigment over any other. Black is a couture look and is timeless. Black is a woman's best friend in terms of minimizing the body, and expressing class and elegance in general.

Smaller to medium-scale (walnut-butterfly) prints/pattern and spaced-out prints and patterns are worn nicely by Hourglass S. Some prints such as florals are great options when on darker grounds in bright accent colors with the print. Background colors of the prints/patterns are best when in Dark Pigments, termed "dark grounds." The objective is to curve, narrow and soften the lines of the frame, as well as to elongate the Body Shape visually, if you are wider.

CREATE A COAT CANVAS OF WEARABLE ART

A large coat may handle a huge artwork on its back. You could D.I.Y. or have someone else either design a scene, pattern/print or hand paint upon the coat/jacket. The design on the coat could possibly be an abstract, artistic design of great creativity. Think about creating one of these for each of the seasons, and in varying lengths... even if you can only do them every 6 years. You can plan them for 2-3 years and collect the fabrics, trims, buttons, fringe, silks, cottons and wools. Designer fabric store outlets abound as do regular, chain, fabric stores. There are embellishments galore in antique shops, fabric, paint, and upholstery stores. All have items that will help you create your visions. (I found an upholstery store in Tucson, AZ. that has antique buttons tracing back to the 17th and 18th centuries.)

Bright colors in an interesting spaced-out, medium or large print, pattern or a novel, artistic design are a great way to express your personality and/or creative/artsy side, especially through your coat selection. Geometrically shaped coat Silhouettes might be ideal for such expression. A triangle/trapeze shaped coat that flares at the bottom, forming the A/trapeze in a dark, black wool or Spring-weight rainwear fabric would be ideal. Even an inverted triangle shaped coat. That is wider at the shoulders and narrower at the hemline near the ankles could be interesting. The dark/black background color could feature bright-red, spaced-out patterned poppies and is a wonderful idea because the coat Silhouette is a wearable, moving, canvas of *Art. Use your imagination and create something wonderful! Or* you could artistically attach fabric strips from discount fabric remnants, scarf cuts or jewels attached to designs all on the back of a coat. This can be done inexpensively to create interesting looks versus a pricey custom-made coat design. Choices are out there. Only imagination stops you from looking the best that you can and having fun with your dressing.

Figure 2 – Coat Canvas Example

Figure 3 - Coat Canvas Example

Figure 4 - Coat Canvas Example

Figure 5 - Coat Canvas Example

Figure 6 - Coat Canvas Example

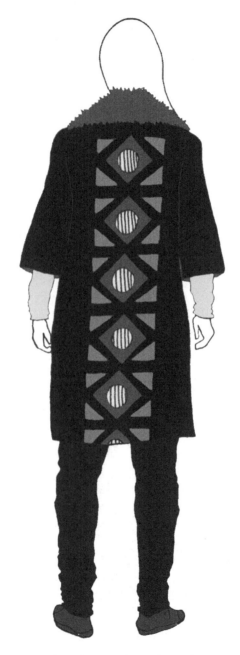

Figure 7 - Coat Canvas Example

Figure 8 - Coat Canvas Example

BACKDROP DRESSING

Another key method of dressing is to select from your BASICS or other Silhouettes in the color black to serve as a backdrop for your accessories, jewelry and themes. These can be a terrific way to bring forth through metaphor your inner *Assets*.

Silhouettes in "hold the body tight" fabrics in black are the best **BASES** on which to create looks. Be sure to include in your purchases and wear your full-length stretch shaper or top/bottom set/shaper. These girdle the flesh in order to "super hold" the body. (With this black, basic canvas backdrop, you are ready to create your looks. You can simply build a look with an Artistic Aesthetic or build instead a chic, classy look.) With this black as the base method you could add a black tee-shirt in a low hip-length (under one of the other tops mentioned). These under tops, near-the-fingertip length tees, become your standard fare and serve as the bottom layer to all your looks. Team them with black trousers, jeans or leggings. You may desire to have another top in a more colorful solid or print layered over it as well. Layer over *that* second tee a longer, leaner jacket that flatters you. Often a longer *and* leaner black Silhouette that covers the buttocks is a great jacket choice. For a change, you may also select a 3/4, 7/8, maxi or full-length coat. All of these options are fun, flattering and interesting to wear. They could be exciting to wear in bright colors, deep pigment prints and patterns or exotic creative Art Canvases that you or someone else design. A good seamstress could make them for you, and is a necessity for altering your clothing to fit your body in the best manner possible. You will always need to maintain fit, and execution of your hemlines and Silhouettes. Take the time to find a good seamstress for this process; I suggest a female, as some items get personal in their fit.

It is easy to select from your key Basics and put a layered look of 1, 2 or 3-pieces in black. This black canvas creates a backdrop for your accents or accessory themes. These accessories may be utilized in order to express your personality or improve your bodyline. You need 1 to 4 separates or dresses, predominantly in black, to easily serve as a backdrop for your accessories.

Figure 9 - Backdrop Dressing Example

Figure 10 – Backdrop Dressing Example

Figure 11 - Backdrop Dressing Example

Figure 12 - Backdrop Dressing Example

Figure 13 - Backdrop Dressing Example

Figure 14 - Backdrop Dressing Example

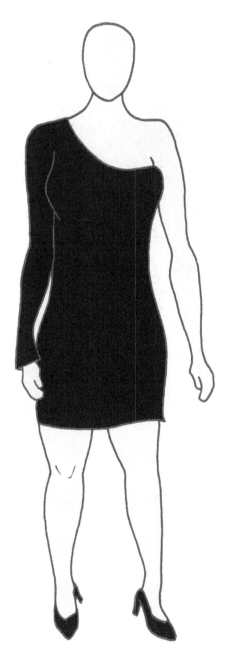

Figure 15 - Backdrop Dressing Example

Figure 16 - Backdrop Dressing Example

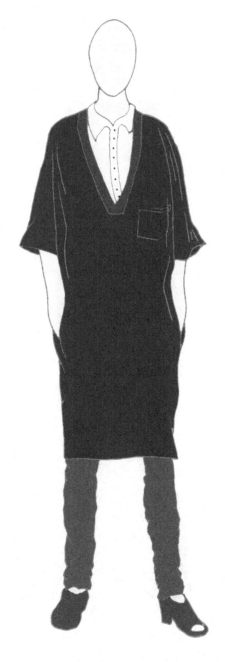

Figure 17 - Backdrop Dressing Example

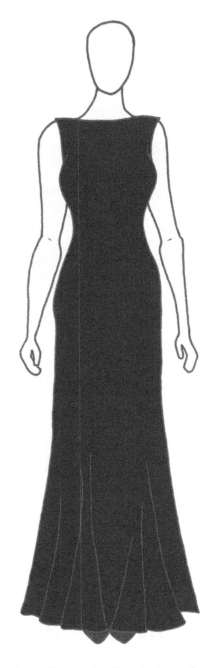

Figure 18 - Backdrop Dressing Example

Figure 19 - Backdrop Dressing Example

Figure 20 - Backdrop Dressing Example

Figure 21- Backdrop Dressing Example

Figure 22 - Backdrop Dressing Example

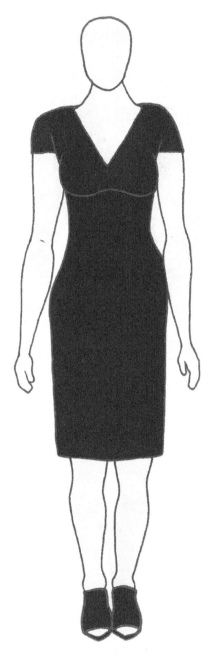

Figure 23 - Backdrop Dressing Example

Figure 24 - Backdrop Dressing Example

Figure 25 - Backdrop Dressing Example

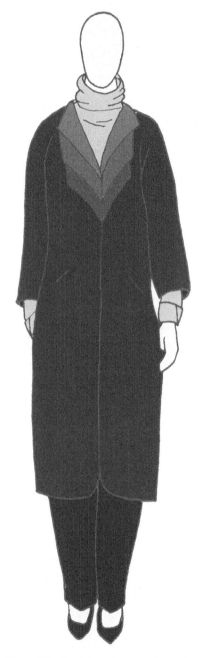
Figure 26 - Backdrop Dressing Example

Figure 27 - Backdrop Dressing Example

Figure 28 - Backdrop Dressing Example

Figure 29 - Backdrop Dressing Example

Figure 30 - Backdrop Dressing Example

Figure 31 - Backdrop Dressing Example

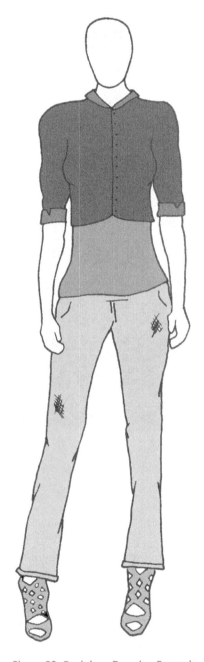

Figure 32- Backdrop Dressing Example

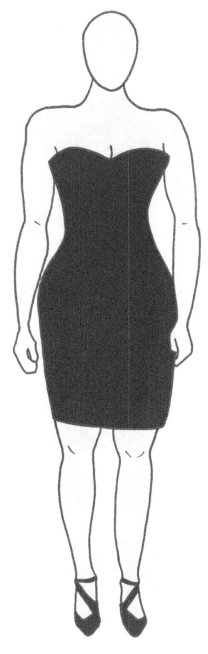

Figure 33 - Backdrop Dressing Example

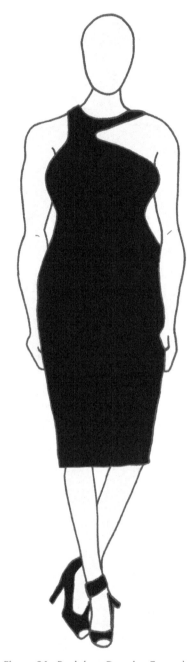

Figure 34 - Backdrop Dressing Example

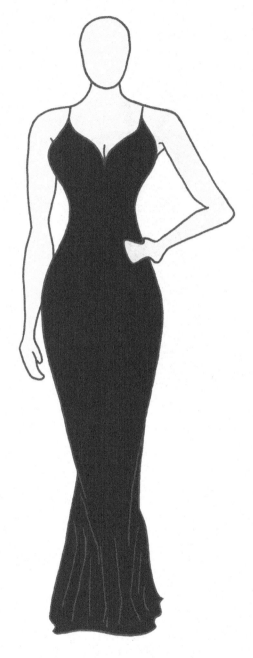

Figure 35 - Backdrop Dressing Example

Figure 36 - Backdrop Dressing Example

Figure 37 - Backdrop Dressing Example

Figure 38 - Backdrop Dressing Example

Figure 39 - Backdrop Dressing Example

Figure 40 - Backdrop Dressing Example

Figure 41 - Backdrop Dressing Example

Figure 42 - Backdrop Dressing Example

Figure 43 - Backdrop Dressing Example

Figure 44 - Backdrop Dressing Example

Figure 45 - Backdrop Dressing Example

INFORMATION FOR HOURGLASS S IN KEY CLASSIFICATIONS FOR YOUR SILHOUETTES AND THEIR DETAILS

Organize your closet and weed out the wrong Silhouettes for Your WAISTPLACEMENT. This clean up job will free your closets of all the wrong Silhouettes and open your closet for the correct Silhouettes for your Body Shape and Waistplacement. The Hourglass Body Shape in Short-waisted Waistplacement usually has longer legs. Your long legs are an *Asset,* and more than likely your shoulders, bustline, face, hair, smile and eyes are, too. Claim your *Assets* and feature them (review *The Guide Book* for ideas on a multitude of *Assets* to feature, both inner and physical-outer ones).

Choices are going to be very easy once you grasp which are the flattering Silhouettes and which are those to avoid. The realization, that "the Waist as a modifier to the Body will be with you for life", is merged into your conscious awareness, you will no longer be struggling to wear the wrong Silhouettes. This is much like a vegetarian who no longer struggles with meat choices, as meat is a NO. You will have your NO's also. Learning the correct Silhouette choices will make your shopping quite easy. You will know how to edit very quickly as some Silhouettes are just always a NO, while others are a YES or are a possibility through alteration. You will begin to present yourself in the best way possible for your given Hourglass Body Shape with your UNCHANGABLE Short-waistplacement. Later in the text you will find **The Shopping List/Recap**. In this list you will be provided all of the Silhouettes you wear beautifully. It is a good idea to keep the list in your handbag or stored in your cell phone for quick access. You never know when you may run into a perfect Silhouette, especially for you. Not that I am pushing spontaneity but when able, go for it!

JACKETS

Accentuate your shoulders through a jacket with a strong shoulder line. Jackets introduce you and are a first impression signifier. Your introduction may make a statement of authority, power, and presence, all beginning with your jacket, face and hair. Even for casual wear, substantial jackets with strong shoulders add sophistication and they are a key Silhouette for the elongation of the Waistplacement. Select a substantial fabric and with stretch yet one that is in no way bulky or boxy. You may choose a solid color or a small (walnut size scale) to medium (butterfly scale) print. Jackets in general, should not be short or boxy for the Hourglass S. Knitted and longer, leaner jackets are the best Silhouettes. Knits, contour better than woven fabrics. Jackets are often available in Silhouettes that are too wide, too short, and too boxy. If they are long enough (a challenge to find) you can easily have them altered and narrowed for best results. If you have shorter or longer legs, or are a short or tall Hourglass S, a great tool is to proportion properly. This is accomplished by making the jacket *length* to at least your wrist. Check your personal Gestalt. Also, low-hip, thigh area, 3/4 and 7/8 lengths are terrific for those who are 5.6-inches and taller. The lower hip to wrist for all Hourglass S is a terrific jacket length. If you are a wider and/or deeper Hourglass S the same applies with lengths, as the longer you can wear them the greater the elongation. Black, Dark Pigments, and deep monochromatic color looks, as well as same-color-looks, are the best choices. These all elongate the Body Shape, as they do not allow the body to bulk or add width or depth.

Jacket pockets are the best if they are, side seamed and sewn closed, slashed, besom, angled, or none at all. The pockets on a straightlined jacket may break the entire look. For instance, big patch pockets enlarge the hips and hit at the wrong position on Short-waisted Hourglass S. If you are also high-hipped this is a double problem as it is your body's widest area.

Jackets, are investment pieces. The top half of your body is viewed first and frequently. Definitely, fewer and better Dark Pigmented jackets are smart choices. Accentuate your shoulders and they will give you presence. Have your jackets finely tuned into a straight lined, leaner and longer Silhouette with substantial yet not exaggerated shoulders. Be certain they do not nip weirdly near your hipbones as your Short-waist is out of scale with most jacket waistlines on the market today. Be sure you have a black jacket, and later add other Darker Pigments such as brown, navy-blue, or other colors that compliment your skin and hair, for Fall/Winter and for Spring/Summer Seasons. Be sure your seamstress takes all the additional fabric and width out of the jacket line such as underarms, and the small-of-the-back in order to have it hang straight and lean. This is not the area to skimp with your money. Your career, your date, your power luncheon, your life will benefit from these "above the table in the boardroom, and office" **jackets**. There are a multitude of shoulder types (the list of types are found in the *Shoulder Styles* in the **Shopping List** below this text). There are many varieties for a spectacular shoulder expression and shoulderline. It may be curved, arched or square but it needs to make a statement. It should not be too obviously over-scaled unless this is the in-trend you want). Select a fabric such as a black stretch knit or a stretch wool/cotton gabardine for daily wear. Make certain the fabric is not stiff, boxy or too bulky but heavy enough to hold its shape as you stretch and move. There is usually upper body weight in Hourglass S and much movement to be sustained by the jacket. For the purpose of this jacket, do not select a fragile fabric, as it will not hold up to the stress put upon it through multiple wearings. If you have to make a choice, have the trousers/skirts underpriced and splurge on the jacket Silhouette. When you can afford to upgrade your bottoms, do so. The section of the proper fabrics in your Silhouettes for work and other occasions is serious business in the wardrobe collecting process. Jackets can make or break your Body Shape and Waistplacement, as well as your looks. They need to stand the test of time; it is usually a **nine-year investment**. It is a major purchase and involves a sizable amount of money in order to obtain the perfect jacket for your Body Shape and Waistplacement, but it is worth it. The straighterlined cut needs to be to the wrinkles at your wrist (longer if you are with longer legs or taller). Take your time and search for these **perfect lines** for your straight jacket Silhouette.

In creating a skirtsuit or pantsuit the skirt and trousers are best if simpler, with back or side zippers, and no pockets. You may choose side-seamed, sewn-closed, slanted, angled, or besom pockets. But having no details at all on the jacket helps it to elongate the body.

TROUSERS AND JEANS
The best Silhouettes in trousers and jeans are: fitted and flared, bootcut, simple flares, wider legged trousers, or dramatically fitted to the knee and then flared Silhouettes. These all tend to balance the Hourglass Body Shape well. Watch for visual depth and width added through color and patterns/prints. All are best with dark solid colored bottoms, and monochromatic colored wrist length Jackets and Tops coordinated over them. Wear stilettos and tall, over-the-knee boots, or ankle boots. Pointed-toes can be seen under the flares of the trousers or jeans, which elongate the Body Shape and Waistplacement. Pointed-toes are deamed the power shoe. They should match the bottoms in color for further elongation. If you are narrow and tall, have fun with shoes, as you do not need them for elongation purposes because you have long legs. If you are wider and deeper, opt for deep pigments and coordinate them to your hosiery, shoes/booties/boots, and to your trousers/jeans/skirts for a longer bodyline. These are usually the best in black and Darker Pigments, as they elongate the entire Body Shape and visually elongate the legs. The dark schemes work very well for the wider and/or deeper Hourglasses. Hourglass S may wear shorter boots or booties as you have longer legs (if you are one of the few that do not have longer legs, please disregard or opt to wear them with opaques as a novelty, on occasion but not for daily attire). Zippers are best if they are on the same side or on back for the smoothest layering.

As you can visualize from above, the longer, leaner trousers/jeans worn with a flare at the hem and in deep, Dark Pigments are a wise choice for the deeper and/or wider Hourglass S. Jackets, sweaters/tops are best in all the same (or near same) color pigment of the jeans/trouser to finish your look in monochromatic color scheme. This elongates the bodyline for the wider and/or deeper Hourglass S.

In order to create longer legs, you may wear longer, leaner trousers that hang with ease straight from the hip, or straight legged, bootcuts, slightly tapered, flared, or more dramatically fitted and flared trousers or jeans. All are good choices. If your legs are larger and/or muscular, skinny jeans may make you appear larger or thicker. If you desire to wear skinny jeans, trousers or leggings, select those with more stretch in a dark deep pigment such as black. They are best worn with the **same color** over-the-knee boots, tall boots or stilettos. Team these with a longer, leaner top and jacket that completely cover the crotch and buttocks. A dark long line creates and elongates the Body Shape and Waistplacement. Deep pigments elongate the Body Shape. Longer boots and the longer leaner tops/jackets help create a longer bodyline by keeping the eye from breaking. Higher heels always help to elongate the legs and improve the height.

SKIRTS

Skirts as separates need to be with flat fronts, due to the fact that the tee-shirts, tops and jackets ALL must be left on the outside. They must be to the hip or longer with or without a hip belt. The fronts need to be flat and the Waistbands contoured or flat. The skirts may be stitched-down-pleating, tulipped, or scalloped. Skirt body embellishments all tend to add softness when worn by Hourglass S. The hemlines of a fluttery, flirty, flippy nature add softness, shape and vibrancy on any Hourglass S, as is befitting to her girly, sexy, curvy, female, feminine body image. If you are wider and/or deeper, the skirts are still a viable option. Carry them off in an array of solids, prints and pattern. Hem them to a great length on your leg. In skirts, color is fun to play with, so choose color when possible. Also, embellishment of all types can be interesting on skirts in any color. Check self-color for adding height and narrowness, as this could be the best option for you. Otherwise, there are no limits on color, patterns, stitching, beading and other worked details on skirt bodies. Skirts can be a creative outlet for all widths and depths of Hourglass S. You have longer legs so you can handle more volume. Keep the waistbands flat as all tops must be layered over the waistband, and fall to the thigh or hip area. This is to help create a longer bodyline and to skew the Waistplacement.

Skirtsuits and pantsuits all-in-one color add length to the body and make your Hourglass S appear longer, leaner and taller. They also skew Waistplacement when the jacket is in the flattering longer, leaner length.

DRESSES

Dresses without a Waistline and with a higher neckline such as a jewel, crew neckline, will elongate the torso and Waist as the bodyline become neckline to hemline. Waistless dresses draw attention to other *Assets* such as the face, eyes, smile, hair or legs rather than the Waistline. If your neck is short, you may prefer a u-shaped, vee-ed or sweetheart neckline. No-Waistline dresses are shifts, chemises, sheaths and floats. Knits and matte jersey are the wisest choices in fabrics. Dropped-waisted are a good idea for day or evening.

Longer and leaner maxi dresses can work nicely and add length to the wider and deeper Hourglass. They simply look divine on the average to smaller Hourglass S. No-Waistlines and ankle lengths are the best longer lengths for Hourglass. Colors best for minimization are best in solid dark colors or small to medium-scale prints/patterns or abstract, spaced-out patterns/prints on dark grounds.

Longer and leaner maxi dresses without Waistlines can work nicely and add length to the Body Shape and Waistplacement, when worn in solid dark colors or small to medium-scale prints/patterns or abstract, spaced-out patterns/prints with dark grounds.

You have options as an Hourglass S. Be sure to remember to focus on your innate and visual *Assets.*

If you choose to add swing, fluidity and femininity opt for ruffled edges, and lettuced, scalloped, or tuliped hemlines in your skirts, dresses, and trousers, when possible.

SHAPE-SHIFTERS

Shape-Shifters are a viable option as these have curved or straight inset panels. If you select the Hourglass inset panels your Body is visually, *Shape-Shifted* into an Hourglass Body Shape. Hourglass can purchase these to become narrower, or if narrow, they may purchase them to appear even curvier. *Shape-Shifters* in knits are great for creating a narrower Hourglass S or to elongate a wider Hourglass. *Shape-Shifters* are best when the grounds are black.

ADVANCED ILLUSION *SHAPE-SHIFTERS*
Hourglasses may opt for the Advanced Illusion *Shape-Shifters* that are custom designed for you to mold your shape into a narrower (if necessary), Body Shape. They may be designed to make you appear shapelier, curvier, longer and leaner, narrower or less deep if desired. These mold, shape and alter the visual look of a body. If you are a deeper and wider Hourglass S, it could be a wonderful choice. They may be designed to lengthen your Waistplacement if you do not have high hips.

GEOMETRICALLY SHAPED, ARCHITECTURAL AND ORGAMI DESIGNS:
Geometrically Shaped Silhouettes in dresses, skirts, coats, gowns, and tops are great alternative shapes. Some examples of theses include: A-line, geometrically shaped (triangle/trapeze, inverted triangle, rectangle) since all are without a fitted or nipped-in waist, they look interesting. Check your Gestalt and be sure they are not too wide or bulky or do not add width or depth to your Body Shape.

Also the **architectural and origami designed** dresses, gowns, coats, jackets, maxis, skirts, trousers, or tops may work if the lines are linear and the piecings are narrow, versus wider and bulky. Minimal details strategically placed are the best focus, as all Hourglasses tend to bulk easily. They should not be on bodices or near the side edges of dresses, tops, coats, or gowns, where the Hourglass form is shaped (nipped in Waist, curve of hips, sides of bustline, shoulder line), as a clean look creates the best results. Where you tend to be an inch shy in areas, it is fine to detail, as it will add the necessary filler to the bustline, hipline, or shoulderline. Details add depth and sometimes width. Check you Gestalt. If in doubt, select uncluttered Silhouettes. Skirts with stitched-down, narrow pleats, hemlines of fluttery, flirty, flippy or tulip hemlines, all tend to add softness while keeping the tummy line flat for the waistline to be flat as the top and jacket will be worn over them and left on the outside of the skirt/trouser.

TRANSFORM AND REFRESH OR PURCHASE WITH THE PURPOSE TO TRANSFORM THE GARMENT INTO A WEARABLE SILHOUETTE FOR HOURGLASS S

Envision this scenario: You see in Neiman Marcus a dress that is to die for in it's detailing! The cut is very ill fitting on you, the style is all wrong, it is full length, and a size too big. Please, purchase it anyway! Why? You are in love with the fabric, which is a washed grey-silk organza with a chocolate brown silk charmeuse lining, and you love the workmanship of its transparent stitching detail. So purchase it anyway, and turn it into a longer leaner skirt.

Flowing, ruffled, faggotting, tiered, beading, embroidery details, and embellishment can add glamour upon occasion. Be careful that they do not add bulk to your Body Shape. Placement of details is important so as not increase width or depth in the wrong places on the body. If you like the workmanship you may revamp/restyle the Silhouette with the help of your seamstress. She/he can add movement to the skirt bodies of dresses/skirts when they are fuller skirts or flared, trumpeted, or otherwise fluted. The additions quickly degrade into weight if overly done or overly colorful, unless they are in the correct Silhouette for your Waistplacement and Body Shape. They *can* add variety and interest to your wardrobe without bulking your body, if selected wisely. However, if you are wider and/or deeper it is unlikely that they will work. Some self-colored details such as embroideries or beadwork may work if they are dry and not shiny, otherwise they add bulk. Search for the right Silhouettes with passion, an open mind, and creative outlook. You are a knowledgeable stylist with a particular Body Shape and Waistplacement in mind. Her name?... Yours!

Dresses can very easily be made into skirts. If the dress is the wrong shape but you like the workmanship, it is quite easy to turn the dress into a low hip-slung skirt, a flat fronted skirt, or a straightlined skirt. Skirts are easily worn with a longer length sweater/top and/or jacket. Tops can have skirts added to them to become dresses. Dresses, especially short ones, are easily transformed by a seamstress into attractive tops that then can be worn over leggings, skinny jeans and /or skinny trousers.

Another examples of transforming ill-fitting, yet gorgeous, detailed, dresses that is one size too big, into a skirt: you spot a marked down (80% off), black knit cocktail dress with ostrich-featheres, and a nipped Waist. The Silhouette is all wrong for you but you are in love with the detailing. Purchase this dress! Turn the dress into a skirt to wear with a longer leaner sweater and jacket, and a beautifully curled/wired scarf. Ideal for New Years Eve!

GENERAL IDEAS TO <u>AVOID</u> IF YOU ARE AN HOURGLASS S

Jumpsuits are usually not a good idea. The fit is never correct and usually are an imperfect choice in many other criteria, including bulking the bodyline and the overall Body Shape.

Overly boxy and stiff or overly baggy clothing are usually not wise choices, but may be worn if they are of limper fabrics such as linen, cotton, knits, matte-jerseys and other lankier fabrics that hang nearer the body, not away from it. Geometrically shaped Silhouettes may be worn in this lighter fabric. Check your body width; choose a Dark Pigment for a streamlined Silhouette approach. Hourglass S need not worry about this section, as you are taller and narrower over all, so these geometric and baggy clothing will be fine just be aware of the effect of your volume on your Body Shape if you are wider in depth and/or deeper, as they may add bulk.

Overly worked material such as ruching, pleating, etc. can be too much. Your shape is enough; the embellishment needs to be minimal. Steer away from embellished bodices for best results.

Pockets front or back on trousers, jeans, or skirts all add width and depth to the Body Shape. If you need to add volume to the buttocks, they may be used to lift and round this area.

Large prints and patterns are usually not a good idea as they add width and depth visually to the Body Shape.

Horizontal or diagonal stripes are usually the wrong scale for Hourglass. Rarely on occasion they can be attractive, but in general they visually add width to the body. A maxi dress in a smaller downward and slanted diagonal stripe in a very Dark Pigment may work on a narrower or longer legged Hourglass S.

Hourglass S need be cautious with stripes. Select vertical stripes only, as horizontal stripes all add width to any Body Shape. Remember all tops need to be narrow in width and longer in length to the lower hip or thigh area.

Ankle wrap shoes/booties/short-boots cut the legline. As they create an eyebreak. If you have longer legs, this is fine. Ankle straps or any strap at the ankle cut the line visually as the eye stops, creating a visual linebreak. This break makes the legs, as well as the Bodyline, appear shorter so it is always a wiser choice, if you have shorter legs, to avoid *those* Silhouettes. For novelty, if you have slightly *longer* legs you may wear them with opaque hosiery in the same dark hue as the trouser, skirt, jean, or dress as this is another way to detect from the Waistline and draw attention to your ankles and legs. In the Spring/Summer you may wear them all in skin tones. The idea is to create no eyebreaks on the Body Shape in order to visually lengthen it and have it appear longer and leaner. This skews the Short-Wasiplacement. Use your personal Gestalt. Most Hourglass S Body Shapes have longer legs so it is fine to wear these if you have average to longer legs. This is just another way to detract from the Waistline and draw attention to your legs.

It is good to keep in mind that the Hourglass S Body Shape has a tendency to bulk very easily with core workouts. This can widen and deepen the rib cage (even protrude it) and add bulk to your Body Shape and Waistplacement. It is best to stay away from Pilates and other core workouts. Yoga and stretching are better workouts, along with cardio exercise such as fast walking or walking. Bulk and muscle ruin the shape of the Hourglass S. the extra bulk created through muscle at the abdominal area only creates a protrusion and width that will widen and shorten the Waistplacement.

Empire-Waists and other empires such as shoulder and neckline empires are either gathered at the neck or at the shoulder then flow from there, usually in extremes of short and full-lengths. If you are fuller in the bustline they could add bulk. If you are wider under the bustline, it will not be the most flattering choice to make. You have many more flattering options. Check your Gestalt. If you are a taller, leaner and smaller busted Hourglass S, Empires may work for you.

It is always important to manage *scale* in Silhouettes, details and embellishments for any size or Body Shape. Your personal Gestalt will tell you if the print is too small or large, if the lace is too frail, or if the ruffle is too childish.

CELEBRITIES AND MODELS WITH HOURGLASS BODY SHAPE AND A SHORT WAISTPLACEMENT

HOURGLASS S - Below, in parenthesis is their BORDERLINE Body Shape.

Dannii Minogue
Taraji P. Henson
Melissa Peregrym
Emanuela de Paula
Scarlett Johansson (Borderlines Hourglass B)
Beyoncé (Borderlines Triangle S)
Oprah Winfrey (Borderlines Triangle S)

Plus Size Model:
Christina Mendez

Note: These are only approximations from looking through public photographs.

SHAPE-SHIFTERS **FOR HOURGLASS S**

Shape-Shifters are dresses with inset panels of usually a contrasting color such as black ground and cream insets. The color insets *usually* form an Hourglass Silhouette on the surface of the solid colored dress (with stretch). The curved, inset panels, thus *Shape-Shift* the body into a narrow Hourglass through **Illusion**. These dress *Shape-Shifters* are available in many bi-color combinations. Some of the *Shape-Shifter* dresses have **straight** inset panels versus Hourglassed curves. All work in elongating the Body Shape.

Figure 46 – *Shape-Shifter* Example

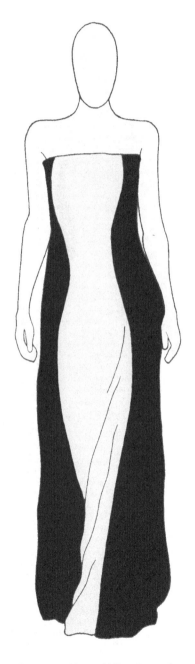

Figure 47 - *Shape-Shifter* Example

Figure 48 - *Shape-Shifter* Example

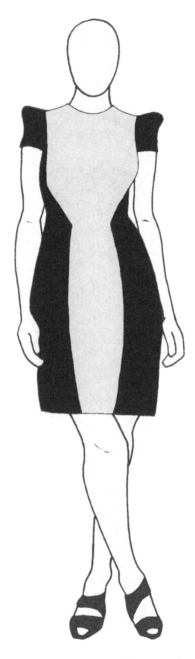

Figure 49 - *Shape-Shifter* Example

Figure 50 - *Shape-Shifter* Example

Figure 51 - *Shape-Shifter* Example

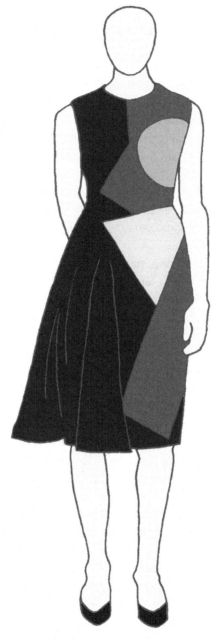

Figure 52 - *Shape-Shifter* Example

MORE UNUSUAL *SHAPE-SHIFTERS* FOR HOURGLASS S THROUGH ILLUSION

FEATURING THE CLOTHING VERSUS THE BODY SHAPE AND WAISTPLACEMENT

Geometrically shaped Silhouettes such as tops, coats, gowns and dresses are a great method to flatter the body and look smart through their embellishment and design. These types of **Illusions** are creations in a very different method of dressing. They take the eye *away* from the body altogether and instead *focus* on the clothing design. In this manner the BODY is ignored altogether. They are a fun, novel, option worn for the pure delight of a complete change of dressing. Maybe the design or Silhouette itself is noticed as a metaphor or extension of your individual personality. It becomes mind *versus* Body Shape for a change.

Horsehair placement, boning, padding, stiff fabric, alternative fabrications and/or molding fabrications may be utilized to *Shape-Shift* the body. Corseting and other *less* uncomfortable ways to *Shape-Shift* are available today through custom Designers and seamstresses. Work with one who knows what they are doing when it comes to creating an improved Body Shape and Waistplacement for your body. You may opt to create clothing Silhouettes that actually *Shape-Shift* or move away entirely from your body. This is actually a quite liberating form of dress type "away from the woman's Body Shape" with the **focus** turning to the **clothing**; these were invented and first designed by Rei Kawakubo for Comme des Garcons and Issey Miyake for his namesake. They have brilliantly designed this way time and time again. It is a very fun, dramatic and comfortable way to dress.

The body's form can completely disappear in ready-to-wear artsy designed clothing. These clothes may be purchased off the racks in many Specialty Stores across the globe and are lower in price than customization through Advanced Illusion *Shape-Shifters*. They help to camouflage the body and may be utilized to create various eyebreaks in order to improve the Body Shape and Waistplacement. The flow-lines created through these clothes are unusual and often irregular or asymmetrical in line flow. This unusual line flow may help *Shape-Shift* the body to appear longer, leaner, narrower or curvier in Body Shape or to conceal the Body Shape and Waistplacement altogether.

IMPROVING THE BODY SHAPE AND WAISTPLACEMENT

With jackets/coats/dresses/tops - It is a great idea to work the *inner* structure of the Silhouette itself in order to visually improve the Natural Body Shape and Waistplacement. For example, this can be done to build the shoulders wider, narrower, curvier or squarer, to straighten the back or improve the waistline through cinching techniques long used in couture. You may have Silhouettes created for you, by a seamstress or a Designer. Men have done this for years in their "padded where it needs to be" sport coats, suits and outerwear coats and jackets. If you are too narrow, too thin or too wide and/or deep, you may have your jackets, coats, dresses, gowns or tops custom made by the proper Designer or seamstress in any *Shape-Shifting* manner envisioned. Your own vision, desire and imagination are unlimited.

Have a Power Suit Custom made for you just as men have been doing for decades. It is good to keep in mind if you are a professional businesswomen the "power suit" is certainly not dead. Owning one perfect suit that has been customized to improve your particular Body Shape and Waistplacement is a clever idea. The selection of fine fabrics, top-stitching and brilliantly engineered inner workings all aid in improving your Body Shape and Waistplacement (and yes, this is very expensive). However, It is a far better choice to make than to own 5 ill-fitting suits. The shoulders, bodice and back may be tailor made to improve your stance in that courtroom or other business meeting of any powerful woman today. Men have always done this; now is the proper time for women to use the customization techniques available today through Designers or seamstresses. Customize a suit especially for you to increase your **visual effect**. These will become your favorite items of clothing. You will feel more confident in your best attempt to maximize your features and camouflage your not-so-perfect bodylines.

Shoulders may also be draped versus padded for shaping purposes.

The cutting of fabric for clothing may be cut on the torso with pins and scissors for a cut of exact fit. Cuts may be designed by a means of linear movement through rectangular strips of fabrics. The linear movement elongates the front and the back in order to create a visually straighter line of your body. This straighter line is appealing from any angle. Cuts may also be designed through draping.

Hemlines may be made to form curves, flips, twists, flutters, curls or fringes. It is your choice, and the vision of you or your Designer's. Various fabrications may be inserted into the linings of the hemlines to *Shape-Shift*. The hemlines move the eyes around the hem or the skirt body in a multitude of ways.

Weights, and other weighting techniques may be used to weigh down various areas of a jacket, coat, gown, dress, skirt, or top in order to reshape and visually improve any area of your Body Shape or Waistplacement. This is also used to simply keep the designed Silhouette in place while on your body.

Strapping may be utilized to enhance, lift, strengthen or hold areas of any given Silhouette in place, while on the body.

Abstracting or improving the Body Shape and Waistplacement may be executed through the use of boning, padding and horsehair to shape and form the fabric from the *inside* of the Silhouette. This is achieved through fabrications and sewing construction. This work *inside*, creates the foundation for the Silhouette to *Shape-Shift* the Body Shape and Waistplacement into an improved visual shape.

An underdress may be custom made with horsehair, padding, wires, boning and other shaping materials unusual to garments such as fiberglass, plastics and metals to *Shape-Shift* your Body Shape and/or Waistplacement. The underdress is then worn under another dress and the result is Body Shape and Waistplacement improvement.

Engineered embroidery may be designed to change size according to the Body Shape and Waistplacement contour in order to improve the flow and *Shape-Shift* the Natural body.

Bias vertical sewing may be utilized to *Shape-Shift* for enhancement.

Lines drawn on straightlined dresses, such as shifts or sheaths, coats, gowns, jackets, or tops may be engineered to visually streamline a Body Shape.

Other more form-fitted Silhouettes in dresses, gowns, coats, jackets, or tops may be engineered to curve the Body Shape and Waistplacement.

Flowing lines may be engineered to flow where you want them to flow. Wire may be utilized and engineered to change what is seen visually. The wires may be designed to be manipulated and bent by you into a variety of shapes, such as a bellowing skirt.

Stiff fabrics and/or custom engineered fabrication may be utilized in order to create a form that becomes a Silhouette to enhance your Body Shape and Waistplacement.

Irregular and/or asymmetrical designed Silhouettes that change with the body's movement may be custom designed by an expert Designer or seamstress especially for your Body Shape and Waistplacement.

Shaped and structured geometric forms may be engineered to remain in their geometric form regardless of the body's movement. For example, a triangle Silhouetted dress that remains a triangle even though you may be a Rectangle Body Shape.

Newer shaping structures and methods are available today due to advanced technologies.

Wired and padded, molded insertions may be utilized to create desired shapes in various formations necessary or desired. For example, spiral shaped wires may be engineered to lead the fabric, creating a desired form such as a waved hemline or a rippled or scrunched skirt body.

Silhouettes created via structure manipulation in one form or another may be custom designed for you. The Designer or seamstress may utilize uncommon fabrications such as plastics, metals or fiberglass and engineer them through more common inner lining fabrications. These uncommon insert fabrics along with the more common ones of horsehair, wires, boning, padding are all viable inserts for molding various body improvements for specific areas on the body. Both common and uncommon fabrications form the under-structure for the front fabric of luxury quality that is the only one seen by the viewer. Their use and forms may be used to create anything desired or imaginable by you or your Designer. Only vision can limit you here.

Twisting and rolling fabric versus sewing and stitching can form newer, different shapes for various body/waist needs.

Colored seaming may be used to draw the eye where you desire.

Origami folding, wrapping, and cuttings in various narrow strips are all methods to utilize fabric manipulations in order to customize, mold and move the body/waist. These alternative clothing designs may be utilized to create Illusion in *Shape-Shifting* our Body Shape and Waistplacement.

Transformational Silhouettes are created due to vision, the multiple fabrications used on the inside work of the Silhouettes and through the cut of the design by the Designer.

Figure 53 – Advanced Illusion *Shape-Shifter* Example

Figure 54 - Advanced Illusion *Shape-Shifter* Example

Figure 55 - Advanced Illusion *Shape-Shifter* Example

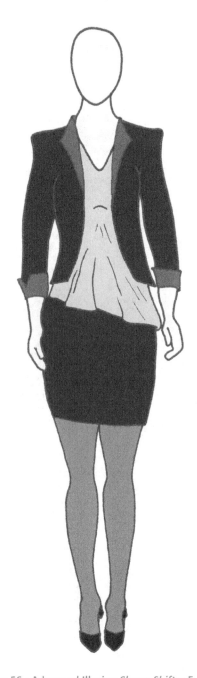

Figure 56 - Advanced Illusion *Shape-Shifter* Example

Figure 57 - Advanced Illusion *Shape-Shifter* Example

Figure 58 - Advanced Illusion *Shape-Shifter* Example

Figure 59 - Advanced Illusion *Shape-Shifter* Example

Figure 60 - Advanced Illusion *Shape-Shifter* Example

Figure 61 - Advanced Illusion *Shape-Shifter* Example

Figure 62 - Advanced Illusion *Shape-Shifter* Example

Figure 63 - Advanced Illusion *Shape-Shifter* Example

Figure 64 - Advanced Illusion *Shape-Shifter* Example

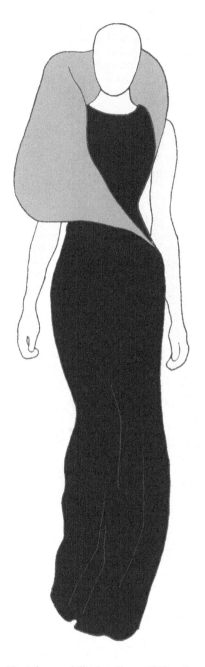

Figure 65 - Advanced Illusion *Shape-Shifter* Example

Figure 66 - Advanced Illusion *Shape-Shifter* Example

Figure 67 - Advanced Illusion *Shape-Shifter* Example

BUILDING YOUR INITIAL BLACK BASIC WARDROBE

This wardrobe is for your work and your current as well as your intended lifestyle. It is better to have fewer, properly fitted clothing Silhouettes than many ill-fitting clothes. It is best to define, think through and execute each of your looks. This is a better method than to just buy things on sale and throw things together with the already ill-fitting clothing in your closet. Keep an ongoing list in your purse or phone of replacement items and needs for your wardrobe, from the tiniest (small snaps) items to the higher priced items (custom coat with wearable art designed canvas on the back of the coat). Appreciate what you have, at whatever priceline you can afford, treat your items with care and respect and they will last longer. You can upgrade your items as the Cycles appear. Create a wardrobe for yourself that is defined with every item selected for each look. Select in accordance with your Body Shape and your Waistplacement. It is best to clean out your wardrobe and rid your closet of all the wrong Silhouettes. Begin to carefully select new Silhouettes for you Body Shape & Waistplacement.

Usually the best fabric for **TRANS-SEASONAL** wear is a blended stretch knit that can be worn as easily in the Spring as in the Fall. You can utilize layering in the Fall /Winter in order to create warmth. Black is a fantastic color to use for the foundation of your wardrobe. Other items will be added into the wardrobe in other Cycles. You may select your jeans in denim/stretch versus knitted or your trousers and jackets in another seasonless fabric choice such as worsted-wool, lighter-weight rayon-crepe, or lightweight wool-gabardine.

PURCHASE THE VERY BEST *QUALITY* THAT YOU CAN THE VERY FIRST TIME YOU BEGIN TO BUILD YOUR INITIAL BASIC WARDROBE. THINK ABOUT YOUR CLOTHING ITEMS BEING PURCHASED IN ORDER TO LAST 9 YEARS, ALTERED AND IN YOUR CLOSET READY TO WEAR AT ANY GIVEN MOMENT TO ANY DESIRED EVENT IMAGINABLE.
TAKE CARE OF THEM AND TREAT THEM KINDLY.

These are the 57 PIECES FOR THE INITIAL BASIC WARDROBE IN TRANS-SEASONAL FABRIC (best if KNITTED with stretch)

See the List below in linear order with Cycles. The **27** for Cycle 2 are starred [*] with details listed for each. Later you can add 2 more seasons to this INITIAL WARDROBE FOR YOUR WORK & FULL LIFESTYLE.

6 - (3 SETS) UNDER SHAPERS of stretch to hold the body tight. (Cycle 1)
*2 - JACKET LONG AND LEAN, 2 for each season, plus Holiday and Resort. (Cycle 1 & 2)
*2 - TROUSERS (easy fit) flattering on your shape either:fitted, flared or straight. 2 for each season plus Holiday and Resort (Cycles 1 & 2)
*1 - PENCIL SKIRT or a fitted, flared, or stitched-down-pleats, flattering Silhouette. (Cycle 1 & 2)
*1 - JEAN, dark navy denim or black knit, both with stretch. (Cycle 1 & 2)
7 - TANKS, for the bottom necessary layer (Cycle 1)
*3 - TOPS/BLOUSES/SHIRTS (Cycle 1 & 2)
*1 - DAY-DRESS (Cycle 1 & 2)
1 – L.B.D. (Cycle 1, then as needed)
1 - EVENING BLACK JERSEY GOWN (Cycle 1, then as needed)
2 - RAINCOAT WITH ZIP OUT LINING AND AN UMBRELLA THAT IS FOLDABLE (Cycle 1 = 2) then, a WINTER COAT (Cycle 2 = 1, other Cycles select a jacket/sweater coat/art piece coat)
*1 - WOOL COAT in black (Cycle 2)
*2 - NOVELTY SHOES (Cycle 2)
*2 - STATEMENT NECKLACES (Cycles 1 & 2)
*2 - EARRINGS (Cycles 1 & 2)
*1 - SCARF (Cycle 2)
1 - SHAWL (Cycle 1)
1 - BELT (Cycle 1)
*3 - BLACK OPAQUES, hosiery/socks/tights. (Cycle 1 & 2)
1 - BLACK FLATS (Cycle 1)
1 - BLACK HIGHER HEELED STILETTOS (Cycle 1)
1 - BLACK HIGHER HEELED STILETTOS TALL BOOTS (Cycle 1)
1 - BLACK LOW FAT BOOT IN A POINTED-TOE (Cycle 1)
6 - (3 SETS OF 2) UNDER GARMENTS (Cycle 1)
*4 - (2 SETS OF 2) WORK-OUT (Cycles 1 & only 2 in Cycle 2)
*1 - DAY BAG (all Cycles)
1 - EVENING BAG (Cycle 1, then as needed)

*1 - ROBE, such as terry cloth then later a warmer or cooler one. (Cycles 1 & 2, then as needed)
*1 - PJ (Cycle 1 & 2, then as needed)
*1 - SLIPPERS/FLIP-FLOPS (Cycle 1 slippers & Cycle 2 flip flops hence forth 1 casual or sandal)
1 - SWIMSUIT (Cycle 1, then as needed)
1 - COVER-UP (Cycle 1, then as needed)

MEMO TO THE SELF
With this **INITIAL BASIC WARDROBE,** you can *leave out* some of the items in your next purchasing Cycle. The next Cycle will be in 3 years as each Cycle lasts 3 years. (BASICS will endure 9 years if purchased wisely in Cycle 1.) Cycle 2 is for Spring additions and CYCLE 3 is for Fall/Winter additions. In Cycle 4 replacements will need to be made of the 57 Basics as it will be the end of the 9th year.

THE FALL/WINTER AND SPRING/SUMMER SEASONS ARE THE 2 KEY SHOPPING SEASONS.
Other seasons are Holiday, Resort and Summer. The 2 Key Seasons (without the need to purchase the Basics that that are on 9 year cycles) leave you with 27 total purchases for Cycle 2 and 3 for your Fall and Spring additions. (Items starred in the list above. Also see parenthesis.)

This gives us 27 plus 57 which = 84, and after the Cycle 3, **111 pieces now comprise your total wardrobe in your Body Shape and Waistplacement.** These additional pieces are added in the 3 years per each Cycle (adjust according to your budget it could be 2 or 4 years for you). The Wardrobe is soon doubled before most all replacements need to be made in Cycle 4, which is the end of the 9th year.

Depending on your work and social life, you may not need to replace your Gown and L.B.D.; if you don't replace these, utilize the savings on extra jackets as they are also higher priced items and big investments. Make a realistic budget based on your salary, job, clothing requirements and lifestyle. Workout/Yoga/Pilates/Zumba/Cycling clothing will all need to fit into your budget.

As part of the process, make certain that you take the time to find the most talented seamstress you can afford. Be sure you set in your schedule the time to have the necessary alterations made to your clothing. In the workplace and in your social life, seek names of reputable seamstresses in your city/town to best execute your alterations. Please remember to take this necessary time and do not leave out this process in clothing preparation that comes post-selection and before wearing. Make your appointment, take or wear the appropriate shapers and shoes. Your Jacket is a major investment item; this Silhouette will be best featured when properly fitted to flatter your Waistplacement and Body Shape.

This plan is far better than buying 30 unflattering and ill-fitting Silhouettes. You need to alter your lengths of skirts trousers, dresses and coats. You need to alter your sleeves on all items. Sometimes shoulders as well as bodices need correcting. Your intention becomes fitting your clothing items to most flatter your body. *It is best to fit them on your body, your legs, your bodice, your arm for sleeve length* etc. Rarely, if ever, are off the rack clothes going to fit you appropriately. Even if you go to discount stores where good labels are available at competitive prices, you will still need to have your clothes altered and hemmed by a professional.

Have your gowns and dresses altered to fit your bustline, your arms, and your hips. Also have the lengths corrected. To enhance your selections, you may change the buttons inexpensively. It is better to have one great fitting pair of jeans, one super fitting pair of black trousers, one fabulously shaped to your body pleated skirt, one perfectly fitted silk blouse, a killer daytime black dress and a stellar LBD for cocktail parties and/or gallery openings than many on sale ill-fitting clothes in your closet. You must align your wardrobe to fulfill what you want your life to be. If you wish to begin charity work or to attend gallery openings, get the closet ready for these events. Pretty soon they will be making their way into your life. If your desire is more time for lounging around and/or working out in the gym, prepare for those. The idea is have ready in your closet what your lifestyle dictates and what you would like to be happening in your life.

Purchase the clothing and have your options in your closet ready to go to any of your desired events that may come along. Don't be the one caught empty handed with nothing to wear when your life shows up just the way you like it.

MORE ON THE CYCLES
In the First Cycle, you will purchase all in TRANS-SEASONAL fabrics; then in the Second Cycle, you will select Spring clothing/Silhouettes. In the Third Cycle, you will select Fall/Winter clothing / Silhouettes. (Fall/Winter costs more, so that time frame gives you extra time to save money). Only starred items need to be purchased in Cycle 2 (otherwise indicated). Some newer items are added to include in Cycle 2 for novelties. Cycle 4 is for replacements. Cycle 5 could be Holiday/Resort/Summer selections and so forth (see cycle list below).

CYCLES:
CYCLE 1- THE INITIAL BASIC TRANS-SEASONAL WARDROBE = 57
CYCLE 2- SPRING CLOTHES = 27
CYCLE 3- FALL CLOTHES = 27
CYCLE 4- INITIAL BASIC TRANS-SEASONAL REPLACEMENTS = 57
CYCLE 5- HOLIDAY DRESS, RESORT CLOTHES & SUMMER CLOTHES = 27
CYCLE 6- ADD FINE JEWELRY AND ADD TO SPRING = 27
CYCLE 7- INITIAL BASIC TRANS-SEASONAL REPLACEMENTS = 57
CYCLE 8- ADD FINE JEWELRY AND ADD TO FALL/WINTER = 27
CYCLE 9- ADD FINE JEWELRY AND ADD TO HOLIDAY/RESORT = 27
CYCLE 10- INITIAL BASIC TRANS-SEASONAL REPLACEMENTS = 57

KEEP THE CYCLES ROLLING
During the 3 years of your Cycle, set aside in a safe place money from each paycheck for your purchases, and plan your purchasing times around key sales for Holiday, Spring/Summer and Fall/Winter. Sales in retail stores or online for women's clothing usually begin around the following times: Summer is on sale about the 4th of July, Spring and Resort sales begin around March and April, Fall sales begin around October and November, Winter sales begin around December and January, and Holiday sales begin around January. **First Markdowns** are the best. It will be very difficult for you to find your sizes during sales. Your best chance is during the **First Markdowns.**

Get to know your Sales Associates in the *key* Retail Stores in which you like to shop. Inform them you like to be notified 2 or 3 weeks in advance of all **First Markdowns**. They will gladly call you ahead of time, and you may even go to the store, preselect your items then have her charge and send them when they are marked down.

Scour the Internet prior to Sale Time; locate which sources have your desired Silhouette selections and sizes. At this time, see if you can engage a conversation about setting aside your size for their **First Markdowns**. When you call close to markdown time, they may sell to you early, but if you wait too long sizes will for sure be gone. Locate your styles and try to speak to a person or be flexible through e-mail and catch it as it is reduced. If you hate shopping in this manner, then opt for the new goods as they arrive. Set up seasonal shopping with your Sales Associate. Have your Sales Associate call you and set aside your favorite brands and sizes. It is a wise idea if you are arriving in a new town (or in your same town if you have not done this already) to set aside a free day (4 hours min) to see the stores and speak to the Sales Associates that will help you. The best advice is to call the Store Manager, Assistant Store Manager or the Department Manager to get an appointment and name of a *key* Sales Associate from your favorite Department or priceline. Arrange the meeting and give some parameters before you arrive as to colors, ideas, purposes and sizes; tell her you will try on things for the Associate to see what fits you, etc. While you are in the appointment, your associate will begin to see your taste and Style Aesthetic, and this will aid her in setting aside Silhouettes for you in the future. Share your Body Shape and Waistplacement Profile and let her see for herself what flatters your Body Shape and Waistplacement. Have her contact you by phone, text or e-mail for markdowns all according to your preferences.

FORMULAS FOR THE HOURGLASS S = S4, S3, S2, and S1

FORMULAS, as you recall, from *The Guide Book*, are the eyebreaks or clothing linebreaks created through hemlines. These breaks may be utilized to enhance the Body Shape and the Waistplacement.

Layering is a common form of dressing and putting our looks together. It may be used to improve the Body Shape and Waistplacement. Layers create eyebreaks through their hemlines. Eyebreaks are also created through details like white collars and cuffs or as for example white lines running across a black dress, a shoeline or collarline may create an eyebreak. These eyebreaks may be utilized to inform the viewer in interesting ways, we are able to visually, elongate and slim the Body Shape, create more curve or take away width and depth through the use of layers. It is all about the eyebreaks and mostly the informing is created through layers of clothing with their multiple hemlines creating these eyebreaks. When the eye breaks, the continuum is lost. This may be a tool or a hindrance. If you want the eye to flow linearly you do not want a distraction to move the eye another direction. If you want curve you need curvilinear lines. Lines that curve the body while viewing the body can be devised through ruffles, details, curved cuts on jackets, tops and coats. Learn more by reading the examples provided and viewing the illustrations of even more ideas by David Russell. We will begin with four layers and end with one.

Provided below are 4 examples (3 written and 1 illustrated) for each line/eyebreak (S1, S2, S3, and S4).

HOURGLASS BODY SHAPE WITH A SHORT WAISTPLACEMENT FEATURING 4 LINE/EYEBREAKS = HOURGLASS S4

LOOK 1 FOR HOURGLASS S4
Jacket: Longer and leaner fingertip black jacket.
Top: Tee-Shirt to the lower hip in black.
Top: Navy-blue cotton menswear shirt with a thin grey vertical stripe.
Jeans: Dramatically fitted and flared dark ink-indigo jeans.

LOOK 2 FOR HOURGLASS S4
Coat: Purple ankle length coat in a matte finish coat with big yellow abstract designs all over the back.
Jacket: Yellow, longer, leaner, straight-cut jacket to the fingertips.
Top: Black cotton-knit stretch tee-shirt, longer than fingertip length.
Trousers: Black matte finish cotton gabardine bootcut trousers.

LOOK 3 FOR HOURGLASS S4
Coat: Brown and off white houndstooth pattern 3/4 length coat.
Jacket: Brown (of the Houndstooth) beltless safari jacket to the low-hip.
Top: Off white and brown, vertical striped, silk short-sleeved, narrow and longer shirt.
Skirt: Longer and leaner, brown matte-jersey ankle in length skirt. Wear with flat rounded-toed boots in brown (of the Houndstooth) leather. There is no space between the hemline and the top of the boot, and no eyebreak at the Waist.

LOOK 4 FOR HOURGLASS S4, Illustrated

Figure 68 - Layering Example Outfit

FORMULA FOR HOURGLASS BODY SHAPE WITH A SHORT WAIST FEATURING 3 LINE/EYEBREAKS = HOURGLASS S3

LOOK 1 FOR HOURGLASS S3
Jacket: Black jacket to the fingertip in length.
Top: Black scooped necklined cotton and silk tee shirt layered over a stretch body suit.
Skirt: black stitched-down-pleated skirt to the below-the-knee, worn with black opaque stockings and black higher-heeled stilettos embellished with silver studs.

LOOK 2 FOR HOURGLASS S3
Jacket: Navy-blue, Wool-Gabardine Jacket with a roll-back cuff in a contrasting navy, black and white newspaper print.
Top: Black, scooped-neck tank.
Trousers: Fitted and flared (dramatically) ink-black-denim jeans, worn with blue snake heels with a pointed-toe.

LOOK 3 FOR HOURGLASS S3
Jacket: Black, cashmere jacket with no-collar and a vee-ed neckline, below fingertips in length.
Top: Black, crew-neck sweater to lower-hip length.
Trousers: Black, wool crepe trousers with an easy fit. Wear boots with a higher heel or stilettos.

LOOK 4 FOR HOURGLASS S3, Illustrated

Figure 69 - Layering Example Outfit

FORMULA FOR HOURGLASS BODY SHAPE WITH A SHORT WAIST FEATURING 2 LINE/EYEBREAKS = HOURGLASS S2

LOOK 1 FOR HOURGLASS S2
Trousers: Grey, lighter-weight gabardine trousers with a straightline.
Cardigan: Straightlined cardigan in a darker-charcoal color. A black tank top under the cardigan is to the lower-hip length.

LOOK 2 FOR HOURGLASS S2
Top: 3/4-length sleeve, dark cognac brown cotton and stretch tee-shirt to the lower-hip or below-the-hipline.
Skirt: Stitched-down-pleated, tan, taupe and coral vertically striped skirt to below-the-knee. The skirt is purchased in a size larger and worn low on the hips to create a longer Waistplacement. Wear no belt or wear it low on the hips, in the same color as the tee-shirt.

LOOK 3 FOR HOURGLASS S2
Top: Tunic (narrow and longer) in light blue and white with red swirls.
Jeans: Black fitted and flared jeans, worn with the same color stilettos.

LOOK 4 FOR HOURGLASS S2, Illustrated

Figure 70 - Layering Example Outfit

FORMULA FOR HOURGLASS BODY SHAPE WITH A SHORT WAIST FEATURING 1 LINE/EYEBREAK = HOURGLASS S1

LOOK 1 FOR HOURGLASS S1
Dress: Black Chemise.

LOOK 2 FOR HOURGLASS S1
Dress: Black Shift.

LOOK 3 FOR HOURGLASS S1
Dress: Black Sheath.

LOOK 4 FOR HOURGLASS S1, Illustrated

Figure 71 - Layering Example Outfit

SHOPPING LIST/RECAP OF THE BEST SILHOUETTES FOR THE HOURGLASS BODY SHAPE WITH A SHORT WAISTPLACEMENT = HOURGLASS S

HOURGLASS S COATS
Keep in the forefront of your mind the magnitude your Waistplacement has on your selections in Silhouettes.

HOURGLASS S COAT SILHOUETTES:
Keep the coat open when you can and wear them beltless (have the belt loops professionally removed by a seamstress).
ABSOLUTELY NO WAIST OR STRAIGHT LINES.
Capes (for day or evening)
Chesterfield
Geometric Shaped (rectangle, triangle/trapeze, inverted triangle)
Military Inspired
Reefer
Steamer
Swing
Trench

FLATTERING OPTIONS IN DETAILS FOR HOURGLASS S COATS

HOURGLASS S COAT LENGTHS:
Micro Mini
Mini
Short
Thigh Area
Above-the-Knee
At-the-Knee
Right-Below-the-Knee
3/4 and 7/8-Lengths
Mid-Calf (If you are 5'6"or taller.)
Tea Lengths (especially the flattering ankle length)
Maxi or Full Lengths

HOURGLASS S NECKLINES:
Chinese
Long and Narrow
Long and Straight
Mandarin
Notched
Rolled Collar
Stand Collar
Sweetheart-Neckline
Tie Necklines
U-Neckline
V-neckline
Wing Collar

HOURGLASS COAT SHOULDER STYLES:
Arched
Asymmetrical
Cape
Cape-Like
Curvilinear
Dropped
Gathered
Irregular
Oblong
Off Shoulder Padded
Pointed
Puffed
Raglan
Rounded
Square
T-Shape
Wider

HOURGLASS S COAT SLEEVE STYLES:
(Embellished sleeves are fine and on a straight lined coat Silhouettes.)
Angel
Art Deco
Asymmetrical
Bell
Bishop

Butterfly
Cape/Cape-Like
Dolman
Empire (under the bustline if you are narrow in this area)
Geometrically Shaped (rectangle, triangle or inverted triangle)
Gigot
Irregular
Lantern
Long and Narrow or Long and Straight
Medieval-Hanging Style
Neck Empire (at neckline)
Pleated
Puffs (mid-arm, and full length)
Roll-Cuff (multi-cuffs)/Roll-Up (mid-arm)
Shoulder Empire (at shoulder line)
Straight Cut

HOURGLASS S COAT COLOR IN ITS DEPTH OF PIGMENT:
You may select from all Color Groups; see *The Guide Book*. If you are wider and/or deeper, for best results, select from the list below.
DARK NEUTRALS
DARK PIGMENTS
EURO-DUSTED-DARKS

HOURGLASS S COAT PRINT AND PATTERN GROUNDS:
You may select from all Color Groups; see *The Guide Book*. If you are wider and/or deeper, for best results, select from the list below
DARK NEUTRALS
DARK PIGMENTS
EURO-DUSTED-DARKS

HOURGLASS S COAT PRINT AND PATTERN SCALE:
If you are taller or narrower the large prints work, otherwise small and medium-scales are best.
Small (Scale to the size of a walnut.)
Medium (Scale to the size of a butterfly.)
Large (Scale to the size of a female hand. Best if in abstract-spaced-out prints/patterns and geometric prints/patterns in any color ground if narrow. If you are wider and deeper, select from the grounds above.)

HOURGLASS S DRESSES

HOURGLASS S DRESS SILHOUETTES: (wear in scale to BMI and height)
Advanced *Shape-Shifter* Illusions (see text and illustrations below)
A-Lined
Artsy-Timeless Designs
Architectural (linear)
Asymmetrical/ Irregular
Car Wash (or otherwise vertical narrow stripping)
Chemise
Classic Greek Jersey (no Waistline. If taller you can carry off more draping, otherwise it can be overwhelming and add too much bulk)
Coat Dress (single breasted)
Draped (be careful it is not overdone or too thick,asr this adds bulk)
Dropped-Waist
Empire (not flattering if you are larger busted or wider directly under the bustline)
Ensembles (matching fabrics and color in coat and shift- dress)
Fishtail/Mermaid/Trains (If you are 5'6" or taller and over or with longer legs; otherwise, too overpowering)
Float (not too wide or shirred at the shoulder)
Geometrically Shaped (rectangle, triangle, inverted triangle)
Halter
Jumper
Kimono
Longer and Leaner
Long and Straight
Maxi
Neck Empire (at the neck. If you are a taller, or narrow *and* smaller busted Hourglass)
Origami Layers (linear and vertical)
Rolled and Wrapped Designs
Shape-Shifter (see text and illustrations)
Sheath
Shift
Shoulder Empire (at the shoulder, if you are taller, or narrower *and* not too large in the bustline. Check your personal Gestalt.)
Straightlined
Tiered (narrow piecings)
Tunic Dresses (long, straight and lean with or w/o shirttail hemline)

FLATTERING OPTIONS IN DETAILS FOR HOURGLASS S DRESSES

HOURGLASS S DRESS WAISTLINES:
Diagonal Waist - Waistband cut on the diagonal.

Natural-Waistline - Waistline falls at the Natural-waist.

Drop Waist/Dropped Waist - Waistline that falls below the Natural-waistline. This is flattering to many as it conceals the Waist position so you may add a belt at a lower-hip length. If wider and deeper opt for no belt and this Silhouette will elongate your Body Shape. The longer lengths in the Dropped-Waists come in handy for hard to fit Waistplacements. This is especially helpful in day or evening dresses, gowns, wedding gowns, occasional dresses and LBD.

Empire - Waistline sitting right below the bustline, usually with a softer or otherwise fuller flowing skirt below. The Empire Silhouette is not a flattering Silhouette if you are larger busted or if you are wider directly under the bustline. There are newer empires such as the Neckline Empire and the Shoulderline Empires. They are gathered at either the Neck or the Shoulder and fall softly from there. Usually they are in extremes of mini or full length. Narrower and taller Hourglass S wear these the best. Other Hourglass S may wear them, check your Gestalt with your BMI and height.

HOURGLASS S DRESS LENGTHS:
Micro Mini
Mini
Short
Thigh Area
At-the-Knee
Mid-Knee
Directly-Below-the-Knee
Mid-Calf (if 5.6 and over in height)
Tea Lengths (including ankle length very flattering)
Maxi
Full-Length

HOURGLASS S DRESS NECKLINES:
Bowtie
Chinese
Dropped Back Collar
Halter
Jabot
Long and Narrow (lapel and/or sleeve)
Mandarin
Notched
Rolled Collar
Scoop
Stand Collar
Square
Sweetheart-Neckline
Tie Neckline
U-Neckline
V-Neckline
Wadded Collar
Wing Collar

HOURGLASS S DRESS SHOULDER STYLES:
Arched
Square
Rounded
Oblong
Pointed
Padded
T-Shape
Curvilinear
Off Shoulder
Puffed
Wide

HOURGLASS S DRESS SLEEVE STYLES: (in scale)
Asymmetrical
Lantern
Long and Straight
Long and Narrow
Roll-Up (mid-arm and full length)
Sleeveless
Irregular
Roll Cuff (also multi-cuffs)
Strappy
Straight Cut
Angel
Pleated
Puffs (mid-arm, and full length)
Geometrically Shaped (rectangle, triangle or inverted triangle)
Art Deco
Pleated
Cape/Cape-Like
Dolman
Bell
Bishop
Butterfly
Gigot
Straight Cut
Medieval-Hanging Style
Shoulder Empire (at shoulder line)
Neck Empire (at neckline)
Empire

MORE FLATTERING OPTIONS IN DETAILS FOR HOURGLASS S

DRESSES/TOPS/COATS/JACKETS/SKIRTS:
(Wear with awareness and with strategic placement or they may add bulk.)
Embroidery (skirt hems or skirt bodies)
Cut-Outs (skirt hems or skirt bodies)
Laser- Spliced (skirt hems or skirt bodies)
Beading and Paillettes (best in skirt bodies as they can add width and depth to the bodices of blouses/tanks/camisoles/dresses/coats, and they add width and depth to the body).
Ticking Stripes (vertically)
Paneling (linear on skirts/trousers/jeans)
Long fringed layers and all over fringed front and back. (They are best when the skirts, etc. are long for the full effect of the fringes).
Self- fabricated flowers appliqued or otherwise attached strategically on hemlines or skirt bodies.

HOURGLASS S DRESS COLOR AND ITS DEPTH OF PIGMENT:
You may select from all Color Groups; see *The Guide Book*. If you are wider and/or deeper, for best results, select from the list below.
DARK PIGMENTS
EURO-DUSTED-DARKS
DARK NEUTRALS

HOURGLASS S DRESS PRINT AND PATTERN GROUNDS:
You may select from all Color Groups; see *The Guide Book*. If you are wider and/or deeper, for best results, select from the list below.
DARK PIGMENTS
EURO-DUSTED-DARKS
DARK NEUTRALS

HOURGLASS S DRESS PRINT AND PATTERN SCALE:
Unless you are taller (as for example 5'8" and over) the large print/pattern is off limits. The narrower and shorter women of 5"6" and over may be able to wear successfully the large-scale spaced-out print/patterns.
Small (Scale to the size of a walnut.)
Medium (Scale to the size of a butterfly.)
Large (Scale to the size of a female hand. Best if in abstract-spaced-out prints/patterns and geometric prints/patterns.)

HOURGLASS S JACKETS

HOURGLASS S JACKET SILHOUETTES:
(Scale to your body size, BMI and height. Have linear movement in piecings, and no stiff or boxy Silhouettes. Longer and leaner is the best).
Straight Lined
A-Lined
Asymmetrical (linear)
Irregular (linear)
Architectural Shapes (and detailing when its engineered linearly)
Longer and Leaner
Origami Worked (leaner and vertically engineered)
Tiered (if linear and small in piecings)
Trench (No belt with loops, professionally removed. Not good if the back flys and flaps at the Waist.)
Military Inspired
Capes (for day or evening)
Swing and Back Pleated Swing
Tie-Neckline
Geometrically Shaped (rectangle, triangle/trapeze, inverted triangle)

FLATTERING OPTIONS IN DETAILS FOR HOURGLASS S JACKETS

HOURGLASS S JACKET NECKLINES:
Notched
Chinese
Mandarin
Wing Collar
Dropped Back Collar
Long and Narrow (lapel or collar)
Jabot
Rolled Collar
Bowtie
Stand Collar
V-Neckline
U-Neckline
Tie-Neckline
Wadded Collar

HOURGLASS S JACKET LENGTHS: (longer is better)
Shrug-under the bustline (cautiously, upon rare occasions and in knits)
Low-Hip
Fingertip
3/4 and 7/8 Lengths
Tea Lengths (including ankle)
Mid-Calf (if over 5'6.5")
Maxi
Full Length

HOURGLASS S JACKET SHOULDER STYLES:
All designed shoulders are terrific on an Hourglass S. Wear them in an array of solid colors as well as prints and patterns. If you are average or wider and/or deeper the Darker Pigmentations will elongate the body best. I would not wear an undefined shoulder as the shoulder sets the tone for the body. It is an introduction to your body and yourself.

If you are wider and deeper watch the scale of your jackets, and have them leaned and narrowed in the proper areas by a seamstress. You may need to purchase larger sizes to accommodate your bustline or buttocks, and this accommodation will result in a jacket that is too large for your narrower, small backline. In this case, have your seamstress take in-the areas that are wide and hem the sleeves to the proper length. Prints and patterns are welcome. Just be aware of scale of the print/pattern with your body scale. If you are wider and/or deeper, for best results, stay with the Darker Pigments. Keep the grounds dark on the prints/patterns or spaced-out prints/patterns or geometrics. Darker Pigmentations elongate best, and minimize wider and deeper areas. Usually all extra details add bulk to the Hourglass S Body Shape. Look for simplicity in form, and have the Jacket shoulder and its linear shape make the statement. Front pockets should be avoided, as they will hit you at the widest part of the hips. Mixing of prints could work if done with awareness, but they may be far too busy on your shape. Check your Gestalt, if they bulk or the eye moves in the wrong direction opt out of these print and patterns. Longer, leaner jackets may be in any flattering lengths. Remember no large front pockets but pockets may be besom, angled or slatted for the best results.

HOURGLASS S JACKET SHOULDER STYLES:
Asymmetrical
Arched
Oblong, Rounded, or Square
Pointed
Puffed
Raglan
Dropped
Padded
T-Shape
Curvilinear
Off Shoulder
Wide

HOURGLASS S JACKET SLEEVE STYLES:
(Watch scale of sleeve to height, width, depth of body and correlate with Body Shape and Waistplacement as well.)
Asymmetrical/Irregular
Sleeveless
Long and Straight
Puffs
Geometrically Shaped (rectangle or inverted triangle)
Art Deco
Pleated
Dolman
Roll-Cuff(s)
Bell or Butterfly
Bishop
Gigot
Strappy
Straight Cut
Medieval-Hanging Style
Neck or Shoulder Empire

HOURGLASS S JACKET COLOR AND ITS DEPTH IN PIGMENT:
You may select from all Color Groups; see *The Guide Book*. If you are wider and/or deeper, for best results, select from the list below.
DARK PIGMENTS
EURO-DUSTED-DARKS
DARK NEUTRALS

HOURGLASS S JACKET PRINT AND PATTERN GROUNDS:
You may select from all Color Groups; see *The Guide Book*. If you are wider and/or deeper, for best results, select from the list below.
DARK PIGMENTS
EURO-DUSTED-DARKS
DARK NEUTRALS

HOURGLASS S JACKET PRINT AND PATTERN SCALE:
Small (Scale to the size of a walnut.)
Medium (Scale to the size of a butterfly.)
Large (Only wear if you are a taller or narrow Hourglass. Scale to the size of a female hand. Best if in abstract-spaced-out prints/patterns and geometric prints/patterns.)

HOURGLASS S TOPS

Open necklines and vee-ed Necklines are usually the best, but many others may be worn, such as scoops, U-Necklines, and sweethearts. Do not wear empires unless you are small busted and narrow under the bustline. Cuff and collar adornment is fine. If you are narrower and less Short-Waisted, you have more options for bodice detailing than if you are average or a wider and/or deeper Hourglass S.

If you are a wider and/or deeper opt for lighter weight knitwear. Always seek out longer and leaner lines in tops for all Hourglass S. Longer lines help to elongate the Body Shape.

Softness and feminine details, including pintucking, dotted Swiss, ottomans, bouclé's and other embellished color on color fabrics are terrific on most, in the longer and leaner Silhouettes. Be sure these do not add width or depth to your body as a narrow Hourglass S. If you are wide and/or deep these will add bulk to the body.

Shiny fabrics like charmeuse, faille and silk taffeta are not wise choices as they add width and depth. Fabrics that are too stiff, stand away from the body and widens and deepens it.

HOURGLASS S TOP SILHOUETTES:

(Longer and leaner; most all to wrist length.)
Geometrically Shaped (in lighter weight or more draped fabrics only and in either a rectangle or inverted triangle shape. Layer over a longer and leaner tee-shirt, and with straighter trousers/jeans.)
Longer and leaner Sweater Sets
Cardigans (narrow and longer not boxy could be shorter and narrow)
Tiered (narrow piecings)
Tunics (narrow)
Architectural (linear in piecings)
Asymmetrical
Irregular (linear)
Man-Tailored
Scoop
Tie
Blouses
Tee-Shirts
Self-Layered Tee-shirts
Shell/Bustier/Midriff/Camisole
Halter
Tank Top
Pullover
Tunic (best if narrow not wide)
Polo
Henley
Boxy (Cautiously selected in lankier, drapier or lighter weight fabrics. Wear a skinny tank underneath.)
Military Inspired
Safari Inspired
Letter
Fanny
Shrink
Tennis-Set
Twin-Set
*Shape-Shifter (*to narrow your Hourglass)

FLATTERING OPTIONS FOR HOURGLASS S TOPS

Check age appropriateeness, size and BMI along with the appropriateness of the occasion. Keep in mind the smoothness, muscle, tone, and slimness of your arms as to choice for sleeve length.

HOURGLASS S TOP LENGTHS:
Bra Top (If in your young teens, 20's, 30's and are not a wider and/or deeper Hourglass S.)
Midriff (If you are young and not wider and/or deeper.)
Waist
Low-Waist
Hip (low or longer hip, not to the widest part of the hip)
Fingertip
3/4 and 7/8 Lengths
Mid-Calf (If you are 5'7" or taller.)
Tea (including ankle)
Maxi or Full Length

HOURGLASS S TOP NECKLINES:
Notched
Chinese or Mandarin
Dropped Back Collar
Long and Narrow
Rolled Collar
U or V Neckline
Sweetheart-Neckline
Wadded Collar
Asymmetrical
Irregular
Deep Scoops
Strapless
Off Shoulder
Cris-Crossed
Strappy
Wrapped or Surplus Wrap
Bustier
Bra Tops

HOURGLASS S TOP SHOULDER STYLES:
Arched
Rounded
Square
Oblong
Pointed
Raglan
Dropped
Padded
T-Shape
Curvilinear
Off Shoulder
Asymmetrical
Irregular
Wider

HOURGLASS S TOP SLEEVES:
(To scale with height and BMI. If the arms are slim, toned or muscular, you may show them off.)
Sleeveless
Short, Caps, or Puffs
Long and Narrow
Asymmetrical/Irregular
Angel
Pleated
Lantern
Long and Narrow
Geometrically Shaped (circle, square, rectangle, or triangle/inverted)
Art Deco
Roll Cuff(s)
Dolman
Bell, Bishop, or Butterfly
Gigot
Strappy
Straight Cut
Medieval-Hanging Style
Neck or Shoulder Empire

HOURGLASS S TOP COLOR IN THIER DEPTH OF PIGMENT:
Darker Pigments minimize size, width and depth. If you are narrow or tall, see *The Guide* Book for all of the Color Groups.
DARKER PIGMENTS
EURO-DUSTED-DARKS
DARK NEUTRALS
BRIGHTS (if not too wide and deep)

HOURGLASS S TOP PRINT AND PATTERN GROUNDS:
Darker Pigments minimize size, depth and width. If you are lean, narrow or tall see *The Guide Book* for all of the Color Groups. Otherwise, select from the list below for best results.
DARKER PIGMENTS
EURO-DUSTED-DARKS
DARK NEUTRALS
BRIGHTS (If you are not too wide and/or deep.)

HOURGLASS S TOP PRINT AND PATTERN SCALE:
If you are taller or narrower large prints work; otherwise, small and medium-scales are best.
Small (Scale to the size of a walnut.)
Medium (Scale to the size of a butterfly.)
Large (Scale to the size of a female hand. Best if in abstract-spaced-out prints/patterns and geometric prints/patterns in any color ground if narrow. If you are wider and deeper, select from the grounds above.)

HOURGLASS S TROUSERS AND JEANS

Contoured Waistbands are the best. It is always a great idea for any woman to wear fabrics with stretch, and to include the stretch fabric undergarments to smooth-line the body's surface when wearing trousers, jeans or shorts.

HOURGLASS S TROUSER AND JEAN SILHOUETTES:

Semi-fitted, Fitted, Fitted and Flared, or Simple Flares
Princess Seaming
Boot-Cut
Slim, Straight, or Straighter
Curvilinear
Shorts: Jamaica length, Short-Shorts, walking shorts and below-the-knee tapered shorts (imitate pencil skirts)
Cigarette/tapers/jeggings/skinny jeans/toreador can be carefully worn with a jacket or tunic that covers the buttocks completely. (If you are a shorter Hourglass S (under 5"4"), 3/4 coverage of the buttocks may work better for your proportion; check your personal Gestalt. The jacket is to the lower hip or high to mid-thigh. Pointed-toes and heels in shoes/boots/over-the-knee boots, or tall boots all elongate the legs and Body Shape. The shoe/boots are best when they match with the skirt, trousers, dress, coat, or gown, as this elongates the Body Shape. All Dark Pigments minimize the best, and monochromatics work for the not so wide or deep Hourglass. Opaques or stocking are best if they also match the shoe and the bottom worn, this too, elongates. All work if the legs are slim. Always wear a tunic and preferably a longer leaner jacket that covers the buttocks. Be sure the fabrics are thicker and not transparent. Hourglass S has the option, if she is blessed with longer legs, to also wear short boots, or booties with her looks due to her extra long leg length.

FLATTERING OPTIONS FOR HOURGLASS S TROUSERS AND JEANS

HOURGLASS S TROUSER AND JEAN WAISTLINE TREATMENTS:
Contoured
Fitted
Straight
Natural-Waistline - Waistline falls at the Natural-waist.
Drop Waist/Dropped Waist - Falls below the Natural-Waistline.

HOURGLASS S TROUSER AND JEAN COLOR IN ITS DEPTH OF PIGMENT:
There are no real limits in color selection. See *The Guide Book* for all Color Groups. If you are average or wider and/or deeper, for best results, select from the list below.
DARK PIGMENTS
EURO-DUSTED-DARKS
DARK NEUTRALS

HOURGLASS S TROUSERS AND JEANS PRINT AND PATTERN GROUNDS:
There are no boundaries, except for the scale of the body to the print scale. If you are taller, or narrow and shorter, it is fine to wear large prints, patterns, or geometrics. See *The Guide Book* for all Color Groups. Darker grounds are the best choices if you are average or wider and/or deeper. Select from the list below for best results.
EURO-DUSTED-DARKS
DARK NEUTRALS
DARK PIGMENTS

HOURGLASS S TROUSER AND JEAN PRINT AND PATTERN SCALE:
Small (Scale to the size of a walnut.)
Medium (Scale to the size of a butterfly.)
Large (Scale to the size of a female hand. Best if in abstract-spaced-out prints/patterns and geometric prints/patterns.)
Only use large-scale if you are tall or if you are narrow. This includes short and narrow.

HOURGLASS S SKIRTS

There are a multitude of sweeping, swirling, A-lined and penciled skirts that work beautifully. Your closet needs many and in an abundances of colors. The Waistbands and the skirt fronts must be flat in order to accommodate the longer and leaner tops and jackets that will always be layered over them.

Soft flowing stretch fabrics, gabardines, linens, and cottons are all wise choices (See Book 1 -*The Guide Book* for more Fabric choices and Color Groups, listed in Indices i. and ii.).

Straight cuts, A-lined, stitched-down and then pleated and others are listed below. The Silhouettes may be embellished with lettuced, flippy and/or flirty hemlines.

The idea is to elongate the Body Shape, skew the Waistplacement, and use color to elongate the Body Shape. Monochromatics and Darker Pigments render a longer leaner line. Contrasting colors are not for the Short-waisted Hourglass. The only way contrasting succeeds is when you wear a trouser and jacket of the same, or near the same, Dark Pigment, and the longer length blouse/shirt/top in a contrasting color. In this example, the shirt could be a menswear woven fabric and the jacket and trouser are all in a black gabardine.

HOURGLASS S SKIRT SILHOUETTES:
Architectural Cuts and Details
Straight from the Hip
Pencil
Asymmetrical or Irregular
Paneled
Car Wash (narrow scaled swinging panels or strips hanging vertically from the Waistband)
Vertical Imagery (designs or fabric pieces)
Godet
Gored
"Fortuny" type pleating
A-Lined
Hem Décor and Embellishments
Origami Folds and Cuts (linear)

Kilt
Chemise bottom hems (of about 3-5 inches in depth at the bottom of a straight skirt)
Trumpet
Straight or Straighter
Tiered and/or ruffled (softer in narrow and leaner ruffled, lettuced, pleated hems, fringes, self-appliqued details, trapunto details, and rectangular or other linear piecing)
HighWaisted (it will be covered anyway with the longer and leaner top/jacket)
Pleated (for types see the list below)
Laser Cuts and Madera work
Geometrically Shaped (circle, square, triangle, inverted triangle)

FLATTERING OPTIONS IN DETAILS FOR HOURGLASS S SKIRTS

HOURGLASS S SKIRT PLEAT STYLES:
Cartridge
Stitched-down and then pleated
Accordion
Crystal
"Fortuny" Type

HOURGLASS S SKIRT LENGTHS:
Micro Mini
Mini
Thigh Area
Short
Above-the-Knee
At-the-Knee
Mid-Knee
Directly-Below-the-Knee
Mid-Calf (If you are 5'5" or taller.)
Tea (including ankle)
Maxi or Full Length
Slim Legging/Jegging Silhouettes (worn as an alternative look under skirts. To elongate the Body Shape, wear them in the same color/hue of the skirt).

HOURGLASS S SKIRT WAISTLINE TREATMENTS:
These will be covered by the longer and leaner tops and jacket Silhouettes.
Princess Seamed - Curves created by sewing of pieces/strips of fabric together to flow vertically.
Natural-Waistline - Waistline that falls at the Natural-waist.
Drop-Waist/Dropped-Waist - Falls below the Natural-waistline.

HOURGLASS S SKIRT HEMLINE TREATMENTS AND SKIRT BODIES:
Paneling
Godet
Gored
"Fortuny" type pleating
Hem décor and embellishments
Wraps and Surplus wraps
Drapes
Pencil
Laser Cuts
Fringes
Tiers (in origami, ruffles, pleats)
Kilt
Geometrically Shaped (circle, square, rectangle, triangle/invert)
Pleat Styles (all tiny and small-scale)
Cartridge
Stitched-down-pleated
Crystal

HOURGLASS S COLOR IN THIER DEPTH OF PIGMENT:
You may select from all Color Groups; see *The Guide Book*. If you are wider and/or deeper, for best results, select from the list below.
DARK PIGMENTS
DARK NEUTRALS
EURO-DUSTED-DARKS

HOURGLASS S SKIRT PRINT AND PATTERN GROUNDS:
You may select from all Color Groups; see *The Guide Book*. If you are wider and/or deeper, for best results, select from the list below.
DARK PIGMENTS
DARK NEUTRALS
EURO-DUSTED-DARKS

HOURGLASS S SKIRT PRINT AND PATTERN SCALE:
If you are taller or narrower the large prints work, otherwise small and medium-scales are best.
Small (Scale to the size of a walnut.)
Medium (Scale to the size of a butterfly.)
Large (Scale to the size of a female hand. Best if in abstract-spaced-out prints/patterns and geometric prints/patterns in any color ground if narrow. If you are wider and deeper, select from the grounds above.)

HOURGLASS S SWIMWEAR IN BRIEF

HOURGLASS S SWIMSUIT SILHOUETTES:
2-Piece
2-Piece with High Cut Legs
Bikini
String Bikini
Bandeau Bikini (or 2-piece)
Halter Bikini (or 2-piece)
1-Piece
Bustiers
Mio
Maillot
Strapless
Bandeau One Piece
Monokini
Laser and Cut-Outs
Separates (bottoms and tops that mix and match for best fits, in solids, patterns/prints/spaced-out florals/abstracts or dotted or striped suits)
Swim Dress

FLATTERING OPTIONS IN DETAILS FOR HOURGLASS S SWIMSUITS

HOURGLASS S SWIMSUIT NECKLINES:
Halters (thinner straps)
Long Narrow
Asymmetrical and Irregular
Strapless
Off Shoulder
Cris-Crossed
Strappy
Wrapped
U or V-Necklines
Sweetheart
Scoop
Bandeau

HOURGLASS S SWIMSUIT BOTTOMS:
(Bareness skin is fine for those with a nice skin tone, muscular or slim).
Small
Brief
Tie or string tie Sides Bikini
Bikini
High Leg Cuts
Curved
Triangular Shaped
Thong (if you are smooth, leaner, toned or muscular)
Skirted or Paneled

HOURGLASS S SWIMSUIT COLORS IN ITS DEPTH OF PIGMENT:
There are no boundaries in color for a taller and/or leaner and/or narrower and shorter Hourglass S. See *The Guide Book* for more Color Groups. If you are average or wider and/or deeper, for best results, see the list below for the ground colors, and use the accent colors from the other Color Groups.
DARK PIGMENTS
DARK NEUTRALS
EURO-DUSTED-DARKS
BRIGHTS
MIDTONES (If you are toned, slimmer or muscular.)

HOURGLASS S SWIMSUIT PRINT AND PATTERN GROUNDS:
There are no limits for the taller or narrower Hourglass S. If you are average or wider and/or deeper, for best results, select Darker Pigments such as those listed below.
DARK PIGMENTS
DARK NEUTRALS
EURO-DUSTED-DARKS

HOURGLASS S SWIMSUIT PRINT AND PATTERN SCALE:
Small (Scale to the size of a walnut.)
Medium (Scale to the size of a butterfly.)
Large (Scale to the size of a female hand. Best if in abstract-spaced-out prints/patterns. Only use large spaced-out scale if you are taller (over 5"8") or if you are a narrow and shorter Hourglass S.)

HOURGLASS S SWIMSUIT COVER-UPS

HOURGLASS S SWIMSUIT COVER-UP SILHOUETTES:
(Vertical designs and patterns are the best.)
Kimono
Asymmetrical
Irregular
Origami
Straight Lined
Shift
Chemise
A-Lined
Trapeze
Tunic
Narrow Sack
Halter-Necklined (mini or maxi)
Vee/U-Neckline
Shape-Shifter
Advanced Shape-Shifter Illusions

SWIMSUIT COVER-UP FLATTERING OPTIONS IN DETAILS

HOURGLASS S SWIMSUIT COVER-UP LENGTHS:
Micro-Mini
Mini
Above-the-Knee
At-the-Knee
Mid-Knee
Directly-below-the-knee)
Mid-Calf (5.5" and over)
Tea (especially at the ankle)
Maxi

SWIMSUIT COVER-UP COLORS IN THEIR DEPTH OF PIGMENT:
No limitations if you are narrow or tall; see Book 1 - *The Guide Book* for all of the Color Groups. If you are average or wider and/or deeper see the list below for the best results.
DARK PIGMENTS
DARK NEUTRALS
EURO-DUSTED-DARKS
BRIGHTS (Check your Gestalt; if it adds size select another group.)
MID-TONES (Check your Gestalt; if it adds size select another group.)

HOURGLASS S SWIMSUIT COVER-UP PRINTS/PATTERN COLOR GROUNDS IN THEIR DEPTH OF PIGMENT:
There are no boundaries in color for a smaller, leaner or muscular Hourglass S; see *The Color Guide* for all Color Groups. If you are average and/or wider and deeper, for best results, select Darker Pigment grounds and use other colors as the accent colors in the print/pattern or geometric and/or spaced-out prints/patterns.
DARK PIGMENTS
DARK NEUTRALS
EURO-DUSTED-DARKS

HOURGLASS S SWIMSUIT COVER-UP PRINT AND PATTERN SCALE:
Small (Scale to the size of a walnut.)
Medium (Scale to the size of a butterfly.)
Large (Scale to the size of a female hand. Best if in abstract-spaced-out prints/patterns. Only the taller and/or narrower may wear larger spaced-out prints/patterns with dark grounds.)

HOURGLASS S ACCESSORIES IN BRIEF

HOURGLASS S JEWELRY AND SCARVES:
Your accessories provide you with the opportunity to express through metaphor, your *inner Assets*. It is a great idea to feature select groups or items in jewelry, scarves, accessories and belts, but be selective. You may layer but with caution as you don't want to overwhelm or bulk the body. A statement necklace at the high neck or collar bone is a flattering option. You may consider themes. Have fun with your accessories and themes, but keep them to scale for your Body Shape and Hourglass S Waistplacement.
Watch bustline placement. Positioned right above or below the bustline, most work best at the neckline, as bustlines tend to keep the necklaces from hanging close to the body. If you are flatter chested a longer necklace could work as could a scarf worn cowboy style (veed in the front) or even layered scarves.

HOURGLASS S HANDBAGS
Medium to large-scale bags are great as are clutches for evening. Hourglass L may opt for metallic bags or embellishment in their handbags. Again there are no boundaries. Smaller bags tend to make a woman look larger and larger bags make a woman appear smaller.

HOURGLASS S HANDBAG SILHOUETTES
(Most are available as both shoulder and/or with handles.)
Satchel, Shopper, or Tote
Bowling (round or oblong)
Clutch or Envelope
Crescent
Bucket, Hobo, Messenger, or Mini Luggage
"Speedy-type"
Box Bag
Cross Body
Framed Bags
Flap
Trapeze or Trotter/Saddle Bag

HANDBAG AND ACCESSORY COLOR IN THEIR DEPTH OF PIGMENT:
All Color Groups see Book 1 - *The Guide Book*.

HOURGLASS S SHOES, BOOTS AND BOOTIES

If you are narrow or average in your Hourglass S your choices are wide open with Silhouettes, embellishments and lengths of shafts on the boot types. Most Silhouettes and styles are fine for shoes, boots, booties, or shorter boots. Of course you may also wear the tall, taller and over-the-knee boots. The shoes with ankle wraps and ankle calf climbs are also acceptable. The sky is really the limit for the narrow or taller Hourglass. There are really no limitations, but as always you must pay attention to scale in terms of the shoe/boot to the scale of your leg and to your overall Body Shape. Also pay attention to scale with shoes/boots as relating to their details, color(s) and lengths as those will depend on leg length, height and body scale as a whole. If in doubt go simpler and let the body speak versus the shoes. The shoe design and sole thickness need to marry well with the overall size of your calf, ankle and leg size. Thick soles and wedges are usually not a flattering option unless you are larger boned and very tall.

If you are a wider and/or deeper Hourglass, or if you are shorter, think of your shoes/boots and hosiery, along with the hemline and color of the dress, gown, coat, skirt, trousers, or jeans, as a way to elongate the overall body. In this way you allow for monochromatic and deep Dark Pigments to run together in an elongation mission tonally matching all your clothing Silhouettes. If you are wide and/or deep you may wear booties and lower cut boots, while matching opaques with trousers or skirts in varying lengths. In the summer, wear nude legs and nude heels to elongate from hemline to floorline. If your legs are disproportionately short, opt for longer boots and do not wear ankle wraps, climbers or cages, as they make the legs look shorter. They also create an eye-break which shortens and widens the bodyline.

You may choose any length of shaft, metallics, prints/patterns for your shoes, boots, booties, or sandals. You may wear high heels or flats, as there are no limits if you are narrow and especially if you are also taller. If you are not so tall, make sure the scale and design of the shoe/boot correlates with your size scale and are not too heavy or flimsy.

Keep in mind, higher heels elongate the leg and the Body Shape, which is always a good option in boots/shoes/sandals, if you desire to elongate or just look your leanest and tallest, while being a wider or somewhat deeper Hourglass S. If you are narrow the choice is really up to you.

NOTES:

NOTES:

AUTHOR BIO

C. Melody Edmondson is an author currently residing in Tucson, AZ. Melody had a fast paced career in the Fashion and Retail Industry in Buying, Merchandising, Product Development & Fashion Direction.

Her insight into the way clothes fit the female body, and the fact that clothing manufactured today is in only one WAISTPLACEMENT has passionately led her to promote THE SPACE OF THE WAIST®.

She hopes to encourage the industry to provide women of the world all Waistplacements, including Short and Long-waisted. Her work led to the discovery that IT IS the Waistplacement, not weight, that is the key to dressing well and loving the body you have.

OTHER BOOKS BY THE AUTHOR WITHIN THIS SERIES
Available on: www.amazon.com/author/melodyedmondson

Book 1 – The Guide Book:
Your Fashion Guide based on Body Shape and THE SPACE OF THE WAIST®

Book 2 – Circle Body Shape with a Balanced Waistplacement

Book 3 – Circle Body Shape with a Short Waistplacement

Book 4 – Circle Body Shape with a Long Waistplacement

Book 5 – Square Body Shape with a Balanced Waistplacement

Book 6 – Square Body Shape with a Short Waistplacement

Book 7 – Square Body Shape with a Long Waistplacement

Book 8 – Rectangle Body Shape with a Balanced Waistplacement

Book 9 – Rectangle Body Shape with a Short Waistplacement

Book 10 – Rectangle Body Shape with a Long Waistplacement

Book 11 – Triangle Body Shape with a Balanced Waistplacement

Book 12 – Triangle Body Shape with a Short Waistplacement

Book 13 – Triangle Body Shape with a Long Waistplacement

Book 14 – Inverted Triangle Body Shape with a Balanced Waistplacement

Book 15 – Inverted Triangle Shape with a Short Waistplacement

Book 16 – Inverted Triangle Body Shape with a Long Waistplacement

Book 17 – Hourglass Body Shape with a Balanced Waistplacement

Book 18 – Hourglass Body Shape with a Short Waistplacement

Book 19 – Hourglass Body Shape with a Long Waistplacement

Made in the USA
Columbia, SC
05 February 2022